SECRET SEVEN ON THE TRAIL

GO AHEAD, SECRET SEVEN

GOOD WORK, SECRET SEVEN

Have you got them all?

- ☐ 1 The Secret Seven
- ☐ 2 Secret Seven Adventure
- ☐ 3 Well Done, Secret Seven
- ☐ 4 Secret Seven On The Trail
- ☐ 5 Go Ahead, Secret Seven
- ☐ 6 Good Work, Secret Seven
- ☐ 7 Secret Seven Win Through
- ☐ 8 Three Cheers, Secret Seven
- ☐ 9 Secret Seven Mystery
- ☐ 10 Puzzle For The Secret Seven
- ☐ 11 Secret Seven Fireworks
- ☐ 12 Good Old Secret Seven
- ☐ 13 Shock For The Secret Seven
- ☐ 14 Look Out, Secret Seven
- ☐ 15 Fun For The Secret Seven
- ☐ The Secret Seven Short Story Collection

Enid Blyton

THE SECRET SEVEN

SECRET SEVEN ON THE TRAIL

GO AHEAD, SECRET SEVEN

GOOD WORK, SECRET SEVEN

Hodder Children's Books

a division of Hachette Children's Books

This edition first published in Great Britain in 2009
by Hodder Children's Books

1

A Catalogue record for this book is available from the British Library

ISBN 978 1 444 90079 8

Printed and bound in Great Britain by
CPI Bookmarque Ltd, Croydon, Surrey

The paper and board used in this paperback by Hodder Children's Books are natural recyclable products made from wood grown in sustainable forests. The manufacturing processes conform to the environmental regulations of the country of origin.

Hodder Children's Books
a division of Hachette Children's Books
338 Euston Road, London, NW1 3BH
An Hachette UK Company
www.hachette.co.uk

SECRET SEVEN ON THE TRAIL

[1]

The Secret Seven meet

'Mummy, have you got anything we could have to drink?' asked Janet. 'And to eat too?'

'But you've only *just* finished your breakfast!' said their mother in surprise. 'And you each had two sausages. You can't possibly want anything more yet.'

'Well, we're having the very last meeting of the Secret Seven this morning,' said Janet. 'Down in the shed. We don't think it's worth while meeting when we all go back to school, nothing exciting ever happens then.'

'We're going to meet again when the Christmas holidays come,' said Peter. 'Aren't we, Scamper, old boy?'

The golden spaniel wagged his tail hard, and gave a small bark.

'He says, he hopes he can come to the last meeting too,' said Janet. 'Of course you can, Scamper.'

'He didn't say that,' said Peter, grinning. 'He said that if there were going to be snacks of any kind at this meeting, he'd like to join in!'

'Woof,' agreed Scamper, and put his paw up on Peter's knee.

'I'll give you lemons, and some sugar, and you can make your own lemonade,' said Mummy. 'You like doing that, don't you? And you can go and see if there are any rock-buns left in the tin in the larder. They'll be stale, but I know you don't mind that!'

'Oh, thanks,' said Janet. 'Come on Peter. We'd better get the things now, because the others will be here soon!'

They ran off to the larder, Scamper panting behind. Rock-buns! Stale or not,

Scamper liked those as much as the children did.

Janet took some lemons, and went to get the sugar from her mother. Peter emptied the stale rock-buns on to a plate, and the two of them, followed by Scamper, went down to the shed. Janet had the lemon-squeezer and a big jug of water. It was fun to make lemonade.

They pushed open the shed door. On it were the letters S.S. in green – S.S. for the Secret Seven!

'Our Secret Society has been going for some time now,' said Janet, beginning to squeeze a lemon. 'I'm not a bit tired of it, are you, Peter?'

'Of course not!' said Peter. 'Just think of all the adventures we've had, and the exciting things we've done! But I do think it's sensible not to bother about the Secret Seven meetings till the hols. For one thing, in this Christmas term the days get dark very quickly, and we have to be indoors.'

'Yes, and nothing much happens then,' said Janet. 'Oh, Scamper – you won't like that squeezed out lemon-skin, you silly dog! Drop it!'

Scamper dropped it. He certainly didn't like it! He sat with his tongue hanging out, looking most disgusted. Peter glanced at his watch.

'Nearly time for the others to come,' he said. 'I hope they'll agree to this being the last meeting till Christmas. We'd better collect all the badges from them, and put them in a safe place. If we don't, someone is bound to lose one.'

'Or that silly sister of Jack's will take it and wear it herself,' said Janet. 'What's her name – Susie? Aren't you glad I'm not annoying to you, like Susie is to Jack, Peter?'

'Well, you're pretty annoying sometimes,' said Peter, and immediately got a squirt of lemon-juice in his eye from an angry Janet! 'Oh, don't do that. Don't you know that lemon-juice stings like anything? Stop it, Janet!'

Janet stopped it. 'I'd better not waste the juice,' she said. 'Ah, here comes someone.'

Scamper barked as somebody walked up the path and knocked on the door.

'Password!' called Peter, who never opened the door to anyone until the correct password was called.

'Pickled onions!' said a voice, and giggled.

That was the latest password of the Secret Seven, suggested by Colin, whose mother had been pickling onions on the day of the last meeting they had had. It was such a silly password that everyone had laughed, and Peter had said they would have it till they thought of a better one.

'Got your badge?' said Peter, opening the door.

Outside stood Barbara. She displayed her

badge proudly. 'It's a new one,' she said. 'My old one's got so dirty, so I made this.'

'Very good,' said Peter. 'Come in. Look, here come three others.'

He shut the door again, and Barbara sat down on a box beside Janet, and watched her stirring the lemonade. Rat-a-tat! Scamper barked as knocking came at the door again.

'Password!' called out Peter, Janet and Barbara together.

'Pickled onions!' yelled back everyone. Peter flung open the door and scowled.

'HOW MANY times am I to tell you not to yell out the password!' he said. 'Now everyone in hearing distance has heard it.'

'Well, you all yelled out PASSWORD at the tops of your voices,' said Jack. 'Anyway, we can easily choose a new one.' He looked slyly at George, who had come in with him. 'George thought it was pickled cabbage, and we had to tell him it wasn't.'

'Well, of all the—' began Peter, but just then another knock came on the door and Scamper growled.

'Password!' called Peter.

'Pickled onions!' came his mother's voice, and she laughed. 'If that *is* a password! I've brought you some home-made peppermints, just to help the last meeting along.'

'Oh. Thanks,' said Janet, and opened the door. She took the peppermints and gave them to Peter. Peter frowned round, when his mother had gone.

'There you are, you see,' he said. 'It just happened to be my mother who heard the password, but it might have been anybody. Now who's still missing?'

'There's me here, and you, George, Jack, Barbara and Pam,' said Janet. 'Colin's missing. Oh, here he comes.'

Rat-tat! Scamper gave a little welcoming bark. He knew every S.S. member quite well. Colin gave the password and was admitted. Now the Secret Seven were complete.

'Good,' said Peter. 'Sit down, Colin. We'll get down to business as soon as Janet pours out the lemonade. Hurry up, Janet!'

[2]

No more meetings till Christmas!

Janet poured out mugs of the lemonade, and Peter handed round the rock-buns.

'A bit stale,' he said, 'but nice and curranty. Two each and one for old Scamper. Sorry, Scamper; but, after all, you're not a *real* member of the Secret Seven, or you could have two.'

'He couldn't,' said Jack. 'There are only fifteen buns. And anyway, I *always* count him in as a real member.'

'You can't. We're the Secret *Seven*, and Scamper makes eight,' said Peter. 'But he can always come with us. Now listen, this is to be the last meeting, and—'

There were surprised cries at once.

'The *last* meeting! Why, what's happening?'

'The *last* one! Surely you're not going to stop the Secret Seven?'

'Oh but, Peter – surely you're not meaning—'

'Just let me *speak*,' said Peter. 'It's to be the last meeting till the holidays come again. Tomorrow all of us boys go back to school, and the girls go to their school the day after. Nothing ever happens in term-time, and anyway we're too busy to look for adventure, so—'

'But something *might* happen,' said Colin. 'You just never know. I think it's a silly idea to stop the Secret Seven for the term-time. I really do.'

'So do I,' said Pam. 'I like belonging to it, and wearing my badge, and remembering the password.'

'Well, you can still wear your badges if you like,' said Peter, 'though I *had* thought of collecting them today, as we're all wearing them, and keeping them till our meeting next hols.'

'I'm not giving *mine* up,' said Jack, firmly. 'And you needn't be afraid I'll let my sister Susie get it, either, because I've got a perfectly good hiding-place for it.'

'And suppose, just *suppose*, something turned up in term-time,' said Colin, earnestly. 'Suppose one of us discovered something strange, something that ought to be looked into. What would we do if the Secret Seven was disbanded till Christmas?'

'Nothing ever turns up in term-time,' repeated Peter, who liked getting his own way. 'And anyway I've got to work hard this term. My father wasn't at all pleased with my last report.'

'All right. You work hard, and keep out of the Society till Christmas,' said Jack. 'I'll run it with Janet. It can be the Secret Six till then. S.S. will stand for that as much as for Secret Seven.'

That didn't please Peter at all. He frowned. 'No,' he said. 'I'm the head. But seeing that you all seem to disagree with me, I'll say this. We won't have any *regular* meetings, like we have been having, but only call one if anything *does* happen to turn up. And you'll see I'm right. Nothing will happen!'

'We keep our badges, then, and have a password,' said Colin. 'We're still a very live Society, even if nothing happens. And we'll call a meeting at once if something does?'

'Yes,' said everyone, looking at Peter. They loved being the Secret Seven. It made them feel important, even if, as Colin said, nothing happened for them to look into.

'All right,' said Peter. 'What about a new password?'

Everyone thought hard. Jack looked at

Scamper, who seemed to be thinking too. 'What about Scamper's name?' he said. '"Scamper" would be a good password.'

'It wouldn't,' said Janet. 'Every time anyone gave the password Scamper would think he was being called!'

'Let's have *my* dog's name – Rover,' said Pam.

'No, have my aunt's dog's name,' said Jack. 'Cheeky Charlie. That's a good password.'

'Yes! Cheeky Charlie! We'll have that,' said Peter. 'Nobody would ever think of that for a password. Right – Cheeky Charlie it is!'

The rock-buns were passed round for the second time. Scamper eyed them longingly. He had had his. Pam took pity on him and gave him half hers, and Barbara did the same.

Scamper then fixed his eyes mournfully on Jack, who quickly gave him a large piece of his bun too.

'Well!' said Peter. 'Scamper's had more than any real member of the Secret Seven! He'll be thinking he can run the whole Society soon!'

'Wuff,' said Scamper, thumping his tail on the ground, and looking at Peter's bun.

The lemonade was finished. The last crumb of cake had been licked up by Scamper. The sun came out and shone down through the shed window.

'Come on, let's go out and play,' said Peter, getting up. 'School tomorrow! Well, these have been such good hols. Now, Secret Seven, you all know the password, don't you? You probably won't have to use it till the Christmas holidays, so just make up your minds to remember it.'

[3]

The Famous Five

School began for the boys next day, and they all trooped off with their satchels and bags. The girls went off the day after. All the Secret Seven wore their little badges with S.S. embroidered on the button. It was fun to see the other children looking enviously at them, wishing they could have one too.

'No, you can't,' said Janet, when the other girls asked her if they could join. 'It's a *Secret* Society. I'm not supposed even to talk about it.'

'Well, I don't see why you can't make it a bit bigger and let *us* come in,' said the others.

'You can't have more than seven in our Society,' said Janet. 'And we've got seven.

You go and make Secret Societies of your own!'

That was an unfortunate thing to say! Kate and Susie, who was Jack's tiresome sister, immediately went off to make a Society of their own! How very annoying!

They got Harry, Jeff and Sam as well as themselves. Five of them. And then, to the intense annoyance of the Secret Seven, these five appeared at school with badges of their own!

On the buttons they wore were embroidered two letters, not S.S., of course, but F.F. Everyone crowded round to ask what F.F. meant.

'It means "Famous Five",' said Susie. 'We've named ourselves after the Famous Five in the "Five" books! *Much* better idea than "Secret Seven".'

Susie was very irritating to poor Jack. 'You haven't got nearly such a good Society as *we* have,' she said. 'Our badges are bigger, we've got a splendid password, which I wouldn't *dream* of telling you, and we have a secret sign, too. *You* haven't got that!'

'What's your secret sign?' said Jack, crossly. '*I've* never seen you make it.'

'Of course not. I tell you it's a *secret* one!' said Susie. 'And we're meeting every single Saturday morning. And, what's more, we've got an adventure going already!'

'I don't believe you,' said Jack. 'Anyway, you're just a copy-cat. It was *our* idea! You're mean.'

'Well, you wouldn't let me belong to your silly Secret Seven,' said Susie, annoyingly. 'Now I belong to the Famous Five, and I tell you, we've got an adventure already!'

Jack didn't know whether to believe her or not. He thought Susie must be the most tiresome sister in the world. He wished he had one like Janet. He went gloomily to Peter and told him all that Susie had said.

'Don't take any notice of her,' said Peter. 'Famous Five indeed! They'll soon get tired of meeting and playing about.'

The Famous Five Society was very annoying to the Secret Seven that term. The members wore their big badges every single day. Kate and Susie huddled together in corners at break each morning and talked in excited whispers, as if something really *was* happening.

Harry, Jeff and Sam did the same at their school, which annoyed Peter, Colin, Jack and George very much.

They met in the summer-house in Jack's garden, and Susie actually ordered Jack to keep out of the garden when the 'Famous Five' held their meetings in the summer-house!

'As if I shall keep out of my own garden!' said Jack, indignantly, to Peter. 'But you know, Peter, I believe they really *have* got hold of something. I think something *is* up.

Wouldn't it be awful if *they* had an adventure and we didn't? Susie would crow like anything.'

Peter thought about this. 'It's up to you to find out about it,' he said, at last. 'After all, they've stolen our idea, and they're doing it to annoy us. You try and find out what's up, Jack. We'll soon put a stop to it!'

So Jack went to hide in a bush at the back of the summer-house when he heard that Susie had planned another meeting there for that Saturday morning. But unfortunately Susie was looking out of the bedroom window just then, and saw him squeezing into the laurel bush!

She gazed down in rage, and then suddenly she smiled. She sped downstairs to meet the other four at the front gate, instead of waiting for them to go down to the summer-house.

They all came together, and Susie began to whisper excitedly.

'Jack's going to try and find out what we're doing! He's hidden himself in the laurel bush at the back of the summer-house to listen to all we say!'

'I'll go and pull him out,' said Harry at once.

'No, don't,' said Susie. 'I've got a better idea. Let's go down to the summer-house, whisper the password so that he can't hear it, and then begin to talk as if we really *had* found an adventure!'

'But why?' said Kate.

'You're silly! Don't you see that Jack will believe it all, and if we mention places such as that old house up on the hill, Tigger's Barn, he'll tell the Secret Seven, and . . .'

'And they'll all go and investigate it and find there's nothing there!' said Kate, gig- gling. 'What fun!'

'Yes. And we can mention names too. We'll talk about Stumpy Dick, and – Twisty

Tom, and make Jack think we're right in the very middle of something,' said Susie.

'And we could go to Tigger's Barn ourselves and wait till the Secret Seven come, and have a good laugh at them!' said Jeff, grinning. 'Come on, let's go down to the summer-house now, Susie. Jack will be wondering why we are so late.'

'No giggling, anybody!' Susie warned them, 'and just back me up in all I say. And be as solemn as you can. I'll go down first, and you can all come one by one, and don't forget to *whisper* the password, because he mustn't hear *that*.'

She sped down the garden and into the summer-house. Out of the corner of her eye she saw the laurel bush where poor Jack had hidden himself very uncomfortably. Susie grinned to herself. Aha! She was going to have a fine revenge on Jack for keeping her out of *his* Secret Society!

One by one the others came to the

summer-house. They whispered the password, much to Jack's annoyance. He would dearly have loved to pass it on to the Secret Seven! But he couldn't hear a word.

However, he heard plenty when the meeting really began. He couldn't help it, of course, because the Famous Five talked so loudly. Jack didn't guess that it was done on purpose, so that he might hear every word.

He was simply amazed at what the Famous Five said. Why, they seemed to be in the very middle of a Most Exciting Adventure!

[4]

Susie tells a tale

Susie led the talking. She was a good talker, and was determined to puzzle Jack as much as she could.

'I've found out where those crooks are meeting,' she said. 'It's an important piece of news, so please listen. I've tracked them down at last!'

Jack could hardly believe his ears. He listened hard.

'Tell us, Susie,' said Harry, playing up well.

'It's at Tigger's Barn,' said Susie, enjoying herself. 'That old, deserted house up on the hill. A tumbledown old place, just right for crooks to meet in. Far away from anywhere.'

'Oh yes. I know it,' said Jeff.

'Well, Stumpy Dick and Twisty Tom will both be there,' said Susie.

There were 'oooohs' and 'ahs' from her listeners, and Jack very nearly said 'Ooooh' too. Stumpy Dick and Twisty Tom – good gracious! What *had* the Famous Five got on to?

'They're planning something we must find out about,' said Susie, raising her voice a little, to make sure that Jack could hear. 'And we've simply *got* to do something. So one or two of us must go to Tigger's Barn at the right time and hide ourselves.'

'I'll go with you, Susie,' said Jeff at once.

Jack felt surprised when he heard that. Jeff was a very timid boy, and not at all likely to go and hide in a deserted place like Tigger's Barn. He listened hard.

'All right. You and I will go together,' said Susie. 'It will be dangerous, but what do we care about that? We are the Famous Five!'

'Hurrah!' said Kate and Sam.

'When do we go?' said Jeff.

'Well,' said Susie, 'I *think* they will meet there on Tuesday night. Can you come with me then, Jeff?'

'Certainly,' said Jeff, who would never have *dreamed* of going to Tigger's Barn at night if Susie's tale had been true.

Jack, out in the bush, felt more and more surprised. He also felt a great respect for the Famous Five. My word! They were as good as the Secret Seven! Fancy their getting on to an adventure like this! What a good thing he had managed to hide and hear about it!

He longed to go to Peter and tell him all he had heard. He wondered how his sister Susie knew anything about this affair. Bother Susie! It was just like her to make a Secret Society and then find an adventure for it.

'Suppose Stumpy Dick discovers you?' said Kate.

'I shall knock him to the ground,' said Jeff in a very valiant voice.

This was going a bit too far. Not even the Famous Five could imagine Jeff facing up to anyone. Kate gave a sudden giggle.

That set Sam off, and he gave one of his extraordinary snorts. Susie frowned. If the meeting began to giggle and snort like this, Jack would certainly know it wasn't serious. That would never do.

She frowned heavily at the others. 'Shut up!' she whispered. 'If we begin to giggle Jack won't believe a word.'

'I c-c-can't help it,' said Kate, who never could stop giggling once she began. 'Oh, Sam, please don't snort again!'

'Sh!' said Susie, angrily. 'Don't spoil it all.' Then she raised her voice again so that Jack could hear. 'Well, Famous Five, that's all for today. Meet again when you get your orders, and remember, don't say a word to ANYONE about Tigger's Barn. This is OUR adventure!'

'I bet the Secret Seven wish they could hear about this,' said Jeff, in a loud voice. 'It makes me laugh to think they don't know anything.'

He laughed, and that was the signal for everyone to let themselves go. Kate giggled again, Sam snorted, Susie roared, and so did Harry. They all thought of Jack out in the laurel bush, drinking in every word of their ridiculous story, and then they laughed all the more. Jack listened crossly. How dare they laugh at the Secret Seven like that?

'Come on,' said Susie, at last. 'This meeting is over. Let's go and get a ball and have a game. I wonder where Jack is? He might like to play too.'

As they all knew quite well where Jack was, this made them laugh again, and they went up the garden path in a very good temper. What a joke to play on a member of the Secret Seven! Would he rush off at once and call a meeting? Would the Secret Seven go to Tigger's Barn on Tuesday night in the dark?

'Susie, you don't *really* mean to go up to Tigger's Barn on Tuesday night, do you?' said Jeff, as they went up the path.

'Well, I did think of it at first,' said Susie. 'But it would be silly to. It's a long way, and it's dark at night now, and anyway, the Secret Seven might not go, and it would be awfully silly for any of us to go and hide there for nothing!'

'Yes, it would,' said Jeff, much relieved. 'But you'll be able to see if Jack does, won't you, Susie? If he slips off somewhere on Tuesday night, won't we have a laugh!'

'We certainly will!' said Susie. 'Oh, I *do* hope he does! I'll tell him it was all a trick, when he comes back, and won't he be FURIOUS!'

[5]

Jack tells the news

Jack crept carefully out of the laurel bush as soon as he felt sure that the others were safely out of the way. He dusted himself down and looked round. Nobody was in sight.

He debated with himself what to do. Was it important enough to call a meeting of the Secret Seven? No – he would go and find Peter and tell him first. Peter could decide whether to have a meeting or not.

On the way to Peter's house Jack met George. 'Hello!' said George. 'You look very solemn! What's up? Have you had a row at home or something?'

'No,' said Jack. 'But I've just found out that the Famous Five are in the middle of something. I heard Susie telling them, down in our summer-house. I was in the laurel bush outside.'

'Is it important?' asked George. 'I mean, your sister Susie's a bit of a nuisance, isn't she? You don't want to pay too much attention to her. She's conceited enough already.'

'Yes, I know,' said Jack. 'But she's clever, you know. And after all, *we* managed to get into quite a few adventures, didn't we? And there's really no reason why the Famous Five shouldn't, too, if they keep their eyes and ears open. Listen, and I'll tell you what I heard.'

He told George, and George was most impressed. 'Tigger's Barn!' he said. 'Well, that *would* be a good meeting-place for crooks who wanted to meet without being seen. But how did Susie get hold of the names of the men? Oh Jack, it would be absolutely *maddening* if the Famous Five hit on something important before we did!'

'That's what *I* think,' said Jack. 'Especially as Susie's the ringleader. She's always trying to boss me, and she would be worse than ever if her silly Society discovered some gang or plot. Let's find Peter, shall we? I was on the way to him when I met you.'

'I'll go with you, then,' said George. 'I'm sure Peter will think it's important. Come on!'

So two solemn boys walked up the path to Peter's house, and went round the back to find him. He was chopping up firewood, one of his Saturday morning jobs. He was very pleased to see Jack and George.

'Oh, hallo,' he said, putting down his axe. 'Now I can knock off for a bit. Chopping wood is fine for about five minutes, but an awful bore after that. My mother doesn't like me to do it, because she thinks I'll chop my fingers off, but Dad's hard-hearted and makes me do it each Saturday.'

'Peter,' said Jack, 'I've got some news.'

'Oh, what?' asked Peter. 'Tell me.'

So Jack told him about how he had hidden in the laurel bush and overheard a meeting of the Famous Five. 'They've got a password, of course,' he said, 'but I couldn't hear it. However, they forgot to whisper once they had said the password, and I heard every word.'

He told Peter what he had heard, but Peter didn't take it seriously. He was most annoying.

He listened to the end, and then he threw back his head and laughed. 'Oh Jack! Surely you didn't fall for all that nonsense? Susie must have been pretending. I expect that's what they do at their silly meetings – pretend they are in the middle of an adventure, and kid themselves they're clever.'

'But it all sounded absolutely serious,'

said Jack, beginning to feel annoyed. 'I mean, they had no idea I was listening, they all seemed quite serious. And Jeff was ready to go and investigate on Tuesday evening!'

'What, *Jeff*! Can you imagine that little coward going to look for a *mouse*, let alone Stumpy Dick and the other fellow, whatever his name is!' said Peter, laughing again. 'He'd run a mile before he'd go to Tigger's Barn at night. That sister of yours was just making up a story, Jack, silly kid's stuff, like pretending to play at Red Indians or something, that's all.'

'Then you don't think it's worthwhile calling a meeting of the Secret Seven and asking some of us to go to Tigger's Barn on Tuesday night?' said Jack, in a hurt voice.

'No, I don't,' said Peter. 'I'm not so stupid as to believe in Susie's fairy-tales.'

'But suppose the Famous Five go, and discover something *we* ought to discover?' said George.

'Well, if Jack sees Susie and Jeff creeping off somewhere on Tuesday evening, he can follow them,' said Peter, still grinning. 'But they won't go! You'll see I'm right. It's all make-believe!'

'All right,' said Jack, getting up. 'If that's what you think there's no use in talking about it any longer. But you'll be sorry if you find you ought to have called a meeting and didn't, Peter! Susie may be a nuisance, but she's jolly clever, *too* clever, and I wouldn't be a bit surprised if the Famous Five weren't beginning an adventure *we* ought to have!'

Peter began to chop wood again, still smiling in a most superior way. Jack marched off, his head in the air, very cross. George went with him. They said nothing for a little while, and then George looked doubtfully at Jack.

'Peter's very certain about it all, isn't he?' he said. 'Do you think he's right? After all, he's the chief of the Secret Seven. We ought to obey.'

'Look here, George. I'm going to wait and see what Susie does on Tuesday evening,' said Jack. 'If she stays at home, I'll know Peter's right, and it's all make-believe on her part. But if she goes off by herself, or Jeff comes to call for her, I'll know there's something up, and I'll follow them!'

'That's a good idea,' said George. 'I'll come with you, if you like.'

'I don't know what time they'll go, though, if they *do* go,' said Jack. 'I know, you come to tea with me on Tuesday, George. Then we can follow Susie and Jeff at once, if they slip off. And if they don't go out, then we'll know it's nonsense and I'll apologise to Peter the next morning for being so stupid.'

'Right,' said George, pleased. 'I'll come to tea on Tuesday, then, and we'll keep a close watch on Susie. I'm glad I haven't got a sister like that! You never know what she's up to!'

When Jack got home, he went straight to his mother. 'Mother,' he said, 'may I have George to tea on Tuesday, please?'

Susie was there, reading in a corner. She pricked up her ears at once, and grinned in delight. She guessed that Jack and George meant to follow her and Jeff – if they went! All right, she would take the joke a little farther.

'Oh, that reminds me, Mother,' she said. 'Could I have *Jeff* to tea on Tuesday too? It's rather important! I can? Thank you very much!'

[6]

Susie's little trick

Jack was pleased when he heard Susie asking for Jeff to come to tea on Tuesday.

'That just proves it!' he said to himself. 'They will slip off to Tigger's Barn together. Peter was quite wrong! Let me see. Tuesday is the evening Mother goes to a Committee Meeting, so Susie and Jeff can go off without anyone bothering. And so can I! Aha! George and I will be on their track all right.'

Jack told George, who agreed that it did look as if there really was something in all that had been said at the meeting of the Famous Five.

'We'll keep a sharp eye on Susie and Jeff, and follow them at once,' said George. 'They'll be most annoyed to find we are with them in Tigger's Barn! We'd better take a torch, Jack. It will be dark.'

'Not awfully dark,' said Jack. 'There will be a moon. But it might be cloudy so we certainly will take a torch.'

Susie told Jeff, with many giggles, that Jack had asked George to tea on Tuesday. 'So I've asked for you to come too,' she said. 'And after tea, Jeff, you and I will slip out secretly, and make Jack and George think we are off to Tigger's Barn, but really and truly we will only be hiding somewhere, and we'll go back and play as soon as we are certain Jack and George have gone off to try and follow us to Tigger's Barn! Oh dear, they'll go all the way there, and won't find a thing, except a horrid old tumbledown house!'

'It will serve them right!' said Jeff. 'All I can say is that I'm very glad *I'm* not going off to that lonely place at night.'

Tuesday afternoon came, and with it

came Jeff and George after school, on their way to tea with Jack and Susie. The two boys walked with Jack, who pretended to be astonished that Jeff should go to tea with Susie.

'Going to play with her dolls?' he asked. 'Or perhaps you're going to spring-clean the dolls' house?'

Jeff went red. 'Don't be stupid,' he said. 'I've got my new railway set with me. We're going to play with that.'

'But it takes ages to set out on the floor,' said Jack, surprised.

'Well, what of it?' said Jeff, scowling. Then he remembered that Jack and George thought that he and Susie were going off to Tigger's Barn, and would naturally imagine that he wouldn't have time to play such a lengthy game as trains. He grinned to himself. Let Jack be puzzled! It would do him good!

They all had a very good tea, and then

went to the playroom upstairs. Jeff began to set out his railway lines. Jack and George would have liked to help, but they were afraid that Susie might point out that Jeff was *her* guest, not theirs. Susie had a very sharp tongue when she liked!

So they contented themselves with trying to make a rather complicated model aeroplane, keeping a sharp eye on Susie and Jeff all the time.

Very soon Jack's mother put her head in at the door. 'Well, I'm off to my Committee Meeting,' she said. 'You must both go home at eight o'clock, Jeff and George – and Jack, if I'm not back in time for your supper, make yourselves something, and then go and have your baths.'

'Right, Mother,' said Jack. 'Come and say good night to us when you get back.'

As soon as her mother had gone, Susie went all mysterious. She winked at Jeff, who winked back. Jack saw the winks, of course. They meant him to! He was on the alert at once. Ah, those two were probably going to slip out into the night!

'Jeff, come and see the new clock we've got downstairs,' said Susie. 'It has a little man who comes out at the top and strikes a hammer on an anvil to mark every quarter of an hour. It is nearly a quarter past seven, let's go and watch him come out.'

'Right,' said Jeff, and the two went out, nudging each other, and laughing.

'There they go,' said George. 'Do we follow them straightaway?'

Jack went to the door. 'They've gone downstairs,' he said. 'They will get their coats out of the hall cupboard. We'll give them a minute to put them on, then we'll get ours. We shall hear the front door bang, I expect. It won't take us a minute to follow them.'

In about a minute they heard the front door being opened, and then it shut rather quietly, as if it was not really meant to be heard.

'Did you hear that?' asked Jack. 'They shut it very quietly. Come on, we'll pull on our coats and follow. We don't want to track them too closely, or they'll see us. We will certainly surprise them when they get to Tigger's Barn, though!'

They put on their coats, and opened the front door. It was fairly light outside because of the rising moon. They took a torch with them, in case the clouds became thick.

There was no sign of Jeff and Susie.

'They have gone at top speed, I should think!' said Jack, closing the door behind him. 'Come on, we know the way to Tigger's Barn, even if we don't spot Jeff and Susie in front of us.'

They went down the garden path. They did not hear the giggles that followed them! Jeff and Susie were hiding behind the big hall curtains, and were now watching Jack and George going down the path. They clutched one another as they laughed. What a fine joke they had played on the two boys!

[7]

At Tigger's Barn

Jack and George had no idea at all that they had left Jeff and Susie behind them in the hall. They imagined that the two were well in front of them, hurrying to Tigger's Barn! They hurried too, but, rather to their surprise, they did not see any children in front, however much they strained their eyes in the moonlit night.

'Well, all I can say is they must have taken bicycles,' said George, at last. 'They *couldn't* have gone so quickly. Has Susie a bike, Jack?'

'Oh yes, and I bet she's lent Jeff mine,' said Jack, crossly. 'They'll be at Tigger's Barn ages before us. I hope the meeting of those men isn't over before we get there. I don't want Susie and Jeff to hear everything without us hearing it too!'

Tigger's Barn was about a mile away. It was up on a lonely hill, hemmed in by trees. Once it had been part of a farmhouse, which had been burnt down one night. Tigger's Barn was now only a tumbledown shell of a house, used by tramps who needed shelter, by jackdaws who nested in the one remaining enormous chimney, and by a big tawny owl who used it to sleep in during the daytime.

Children had played in it until they had been forbidden to in case the old walls gave way. Jack and George had once explored it with Peter, but an old tramp had risen up from a corner and shouted at them so loudly that they had fled away.

The two boys trudged on. They came to the hill and walked up the narrow lane that led to Tigger's Barn. Still there was no sign of Jeff or Susie. Well, if they had taken bicycles, they would certainly be at Tigger's Barn by now!

They came to the old building at last. It stood there in the rather dim moonlight, looking forlorn and bony, with part of its roof missing, and its one great chimney sticking up into the night sky.

'Here we are,' whispered Jack. 'Walk quietly, because we don't want to let Jeff and Susie know we're here, or those men either, if they've come already! But everything is very quiet. I don't think the men are here.'

They kept in the shadow of a great yew hedge, and made their way on tiptoe to the back of the house. There was a front door and a back door, and both were locked, but as no window had glass in, it was easy enough for anyone to get inside the tumble-down place if they wanted to.

Jack clambered in through a downstairs window. A scuttling noise startled him, and he clutched George and made him jump.

'Don't grab me like that,' complained George, in a whisper. 'It was only a rat hurrying away. You nearly made me yell when you grabbed me so suddenly.'

'Sh!' said Jack. 'What's that?'

They listened. Something was moving high up in the great chimney that towered from the hearth in the broken-down room they were in.

'Maybe it's the owl,' said George, at last. 'Yes, listen to it hooting.'

A quavering hoot came to their ears. But it didn't really sound as if it came from the chimney. It seemed to come from outside the house, in the overgrown garden. Then an answering hoot came, but it didn't sound at all like an owl.

'Jack,' whispered George, his mouth close to Jack's ear, 'that's not an owl. It's men signalling to one another. They *are* meeting here! But where are Susie and Jeff?'

'I don't know. Hidden safely somewhere,

I expect,' said Jack, suddenly feeling a bit shaky at the knees. 'We'd better hide too. Those men will be here in half a minute.'

'There's a good hiding-place over there in the hearth,' whispered George. 'We can stand there in the darkness, right under the big chimney. Come on, quick. I'm sure I can hear footsteps outside.'

The two boys ran silently to the hearth. Tramps had made fires there from time to time, and a heap of ashes half-filled the hearth. The boys stood ankle-deep in them, hardly daring to breathe.

Then a torch suddenly shone out, and raked the room with its beam. Jack and George pressed close together, hoping they did not show in the great hearth.

They heard the sound of someone climbing in through the same window they had come in by. Then a voice spoke to someone outside.

'Come on in. Nobody's here. Larry hasn't

come yet. Give him the signal, Zeb, in case he's waiting about for it now.'

Somebody gave a quavering hoot again. 'Ooooo-oo-oo! Ooooo, ooo-oo-oo!'

An answering call came from some way away, and after about half a minute another man climbed in. Now there were three.

The two boys held their breath. Good gracious! They were right in the middle of something very strange! Why were these men meeting at this tumbledown place? Who were they and what were they doing?

Where were Susie and Jeff, too? Were they listening and watching as well?

'Come into the next room,' said the man who had first spoken. 'There are boxes there to sit on, and a light won't shine out there as much as it does from this room. Come on, Larry – here, Zeb, shine your torch in front.'

[8]

An uncomfortable time

The two boys were half-glad, half-sorry that the men had gone into another room. Glad because they were no longer afraid of being found, but sorry because it was now impossible to hear clearly what the men were saying.

They could hear a murmur from the next room.

Jack nudged George. 'I'm going to creep across the floor and go to the door. Perhaps I can hear what they are saying then,' he whispered.

'No, don't,' said George, in alarm. 'We'll be discovered. You're sure to make a noise!'

'I've got rubber-soled shoes on. I shan't make a sound,' whispered back Jack. 'You stay here, George. I DO wonder where Susie and Jeff are. I hope I don't bump into them anywhere.'

Jack made his way very quietly to the doorway that led to the next room. There was a broken door still hanging there, and he could peep through the crack. He saw the three men in the room beyond, sitting on old boxes, intently studying a map of some kind, and talking in low voices.

If only he could hear what they said! He tried to see what the men were like, but it was too dark. He could only hear their voices, one a polished voice speaking clearly and firmly, and the other two rough and unpleasant.

Jack hadn't the slightest idea what they were talking about. Loading and unloading. Six-two or maybe seven-ten. Points, points, points. There mustn't be a moon. Darkness, fog, mist. Points. Fog. Six-two, but it might go as long as seven-twenty. And again, points points, points.

What in the world could they be discussing? It was maddening to hear odd words like this that made no sense. Jack strained his ears to try and make out more, but it was no use, he couldn't. He decided to edge a little nearer.

He leaned against something that gave way behind him. It was a cupboard door! Before he could stop himself Jack fell inside, landing with a soft thud. The door closed on him with a little click. He sat there, alarmed and astonished, not daring to move.

'What was that?' said one of the men.

They all listened, and at that moment a big rat ran silently round the room, keeping to the wall. One of the men picked it out in the light of his torch.

'Rats,' he said. 'This place is alive with them. That's what we heard.'

'I'm not sure,' said the man with the clear voice. 'Switch off that light, Zeb. Sit quietly for a bit and listen.'

The light was switched off. The men sat in utter silence, listening. Another rat scuttered over the floor.

Jack sat absolutely still in the cupboard, fearful that the men might come to find out who had made a noise. George stood in the hearth of the next room, wondering what had happened. There was such dead silence now, and darkness too!

The owl awoke in the chimney above him, and stirred once more. Night-time! It must go hunting. It gave one soft hoot and dropped down the chimney to make its way out through the bare window.

It was as startled to find George standing at the bottom of the chimney as George was startled to feel the owl brushing his cheek. It flew silently out of the window, a big moving shadow in the dimness.

George couldn't bear it. He must get out of this chimneyplace, he must! Something else might fall down on him and touch his face softly. Where was Jack? How mean of him to go off and leave him with things that lived in chimneys! And Jack had the torch with him too. George would have given anything to flick on the light of a torch.

He crept out of the hearth, and stood in the middle of the floor, wondering what to do. What *was* Jack doing? He had said he was going to the doorway that led to the next room, to see if he could hear what the men said. But were the men there now? There wasn't a sound to be heard.

Perhaps they have slipped out of another window and gone, thought poor George. If so why doesn't Jack come back? It's horrid of him. I can't bear this much longer.

He moved over to the doorway, putting out his hands to feel if Jack was there. No, he wasn't. The next room was in black darkness, and he couldn't see a thing there.

There was also complete silence. Where *was* everyone?

George felt his legs giving way at the knees. This horrible old tumbledown place! Why ever had he listened to Jack and come here with him? He was sure that Jeff and Susie hadn't been stupid enough to come here at night.

He didn't dare to call out. Perhaps Jack was somewhere nearby, scared too. What about the Secret Seven password? What was it now? Cheeky Charlie!

If I whisper Cheeky Charlie, Jack will know it's me, he thought. It's our password. He'll know it's me, and he'll answer.

So he stood at the doorway and whispered: 'Cheeky Charlie! Cheeky Charlie!'

No answer. He tried again, a little louder this time, 'Cheeky Charlie!'

And then a torch snapped on, and caught him directly in its beam. A voice spoke to him harshly.

'What's all this? What do you know about Charlie? Come right into the room, boy, and answer my question.'

[9]

Very peculiar

George was extremely astonished. Why, the men were still there! Then where was Jack? What had happened to him? He stood there in the beam of the torch, gaping.

'Come on in,' said the voice, impatiently. 'We heard you saying "Cheeky Charlie". Have you got a message from him?'

George gaped still more. A message from him? From Cheeky Charlie? Why, that was only a password! Just the name of a dog! What did the man mean?

'*Will* you come into the room?' said the man, again. 'What's the matter with you, boy? Are you scared? We shan't eat a messenger from Charlie.'

George went slowly into the room, his

mind suddenly working at top speed. A messenger from Charlie. Could there be someone called Charlie, Cheeky Charlie? Did these men think he had come from him? How very extraordinary!

'There won't be no message from Charlie,' said the man called Zeb. 'Why should there be? He's waiting for news from *us*, isn't he? Here, boy – did Charlie send you to ask for news?'

George could do nothing but nod his head. He didn't want to have to explain anything at all. These men appeared to think he had come to find them to get news for someone called Charlie. Perhaps if he let them give him the message, they would let him go without any further questions.

'Can't think why Charlie uses such a dumb kid to send out,' grumbled Zeb. 'Got a pencil, Larry? I'll scribble a message.'

'A kid that can't open his mouth and speak a word is just the right messenger for us,' said the man with the clear voice. 'Tell Charlie what we've decided, Zeb. Don't forget that he's to mark the tarpaulin with white lines at one corner.'

Zeb scribbled something in a notebook by the light of a torch. He tore out the page and folded it over. 'Here you are,' he said to George. 'Take this to Charlie, and don't you go calling him Cheeky Charlie, see? Little boys that are rude get their ears boxed! His friends can call him what they like, but not you.'

'Oh, leave the kid alone,' said Larry. 'Where's Charlie now, kid? At Dalling's or at Hammond's?'

George didn't know what to answer. 'Dalling's,' he said at last, not knowing in the least what it meant.

Larry tossed him fifty pence. 'Clear off!' he said. 'You're scared stiff of this place, aren't you? Want me to take you down the hill?'

This was the last thing that poor George wanted. He shook his head.

The men got up. 'Well, if you want company, we're all going now. If not, buzz off.'

George buzzed off, but not very far. He went back again into the other room, thankful to see that the moon had come out again, and had lit it enough for him to make his way quickly to the window. He clambered out awkwardly, because his legs were shaking and were not easy to manage.

He made for a thick bush and flung himself into the middle. If those men really were going, he could wait till they were gone. Then he could go back and find Jack. WHAT had happened to Jack? He seemed to have disappeared completely.

The men went cautiously out of Tigger's Barn, keeping their voices low. The owl flew over their heads, giving a sudden hoot that startled them. Then George heard them laugh. Their footsteps went quietly down the hill.

He heaved a sigh of relief. Then he scrambled out of the bush and went back into the house. He stood debating what to do. Should he try the password again? It had had surprising results last time, so perhaps this time it would be better just to call Jack's name.

But before he could do so, a voice came out of the doorway that led to the further room.

'Cheeky Charlie!' it said, in a piercing whisper.

George stood stock still, and didn't answer. Was it Jack saying that password? Or was it somebody else who knew the real Cheeky Charlie, whoever he might be?

Then a light flashed on and caught him in its beam. But this time, thank goodness, it was Jack's torch, and Jack himself gave an exclamation of relief.

'It *is* you, George! Why in the world didn't you answer when I said the password? You must have known it was me.'

'Oh, Jack! Where were you? I've had an awful time!' said George. 'You shouldn't have gone off and left me like that. Where have you been?'

'I was listening to those men, and fell into this cupboard,' said Jack. 'It shut on me, and I couldn't hear another word. I didn't dare to move in case those men came to look for me. But at last I opened the door, and when I couldn't hear anything, I wondered where *you* were! So I whispered the password.'

'Oh, I see,' said George, thankfully. 'So you didn't hear what happened to *me*? The men discovered me – and—'

'*Discovered* you! What did they do?' said Jack, in the greatest astonishment.

'It's really very peculiar,' said George. 'You see, *I* whispered the password too, hoping *you* would hear it. But the *men* heard me whispering "Cheeky Charlie", and they called me in and asked me if I was a messenger from him.'

Jack didn't follow this, and it took George a little time to explain to him that the three men seemed really to think that someone they knew, who actually *was* called Cheeky Charlie, was using George as a messenger!

'And they gave *me* a message for him,' said George. 'In a note. I've got it in my pocket.'

'No! Have you really!' said Jack, suddenly excited. 'Gosh, this is thrilling. We might be in the middle of an adventure again. Let's see the note.'

'No. Let's go home and then read it,' said George. 'I want to get out of this tumble-down old place, I don't like it a bit. Something came down the chimney on me, and I nearly had a fit. Come on, Jack, I want to go.'

'Yes, but wait,' said Jack, suddenly remembering. 'What about Susie and Jeff? They must be somewhere here too. We ought to look for them.'

'We'll have to find out how they knew there was to be a meeting here tonight,' said George. 'Let's call them, Jack. Honestly, there's nobody else here now. *I'm* going to call them anyway!'

So he shouted loudly: 'JEFF! SUSIE! COME ON OUT, WHEREVER YOU ARE!'

His voice echoed through the old house, but nobody stirred, nobody answered.

'I'll go through the place with the torch,' said Jack, and the two boys went bravely into each broken-down, bare room, flashing the light all round.

There was no one to be seen. Jack suddenly felt anxious. Susie was his sister. What had happened to her?

'George, we must go back home as quickly as we can, and tell Mother that

Susie's disappeared,' he said. 'And Jeff has too. Come on quick! Something may have happened to them.'

They went back to Jack's house as quickly as they could. As they ran to the front gate, Jack saw his mother coming back from her meeting. He rushed to her.

'Mother! Susie's missing! She's gone! Oh, Mother, she went to Tigger's Barn, and now she isn't there!'

His mother looked at him in alarm. She opened the front door quickly and went in, followed by the two boys.

'Now tell me quickly,' she said. 'What do you mean? Why did Susie go out? When—'

A door was flung open upstairs and a merry voice called out: 'Hallo, Mother! Is that you? Come and see Jeff's railway going! And don't scold us because it's so late; we've been waiting for Jack and George to come back.'

'Why, that's Susie,' said her mother, in

surprise. 'What did you mean, Jack, about Susie disappearing. What a silly joke!'

Sure enough, there were Susie and Jeff upstairs, with the whole floor laid out with railway lines!

Jack stared at Susie in surprise and indignation. Hadn't she gone out, then? She grinned at him wickedly.

'Serves you right!' she said rudely. 'Who came spying on our Famous Five meeting? Who heard all sorts of things and believed them? Who's been all the way to Tigger's Barn in the dark? Who's a silly-billy, who's a—'

Jack rushed at her in a rage. She dodged behind her mother, laughing.

'Now, Jack, now!' said his mother. 'Stop that, please. What has been happening? Susie, go to bed. Jeff, clear up your lines. It's time for you to go. Your mother will be telephoning to ask why you are not home. JACK! Did you hear what I said? Leave Susie alone.'

Jeff went to take up his lines, and George helped him. Both boys were scared of Jack's mother when she was cross. Susie ran to her room and slammed the door.

'She's a wicked girl,' raged Jack, 'she – she – she . . .'

'Go and turn on the bath-water,' said his mother, sharply. 'You can both go without your supper now. I WILL NOT have this behaviour.'

George and Jeff disappeared out of the house as quickly as they could, carrying the boxes of railway things. George completely forgot what he had in his pocket – a pencilled note to someone called Cheeky Charlie, which he hadn't even read! Well, well, well!

[10]

Call a meeting!

George went quickly along the road with Jeff. Jeff chuckled.

'I say, you and Jack fell for our little trick beautifully, didn't you? Susie's clever, she laid her plan well. We all talked at the tops of our voices so that Jack would be sure to hear. We knew he was hiding in the laurel bush.'

George said nothing. He was angry that Susie and the Famous Five should have played a trick like that on the Secret Seven – angry that Jack had been so easily taken in – but, dear me, what curious results that trick had had!

Susie had mentioned Tigger's Barn just to make Jack and the Secret Seven think that the Famous Five had got hold of something that was going on there, and had talked about a make-believe Stumpy Dick and Twisty Tom. And lo and behold, something *was* going on there, not between Stumpy Dick and Twisty Tom, but between three mysterious fellows called Zeb, Larry, and had he heard the other man's name? No, he hadn't.

'You're quiet, George,' said Jeff, chuckling again. 'How did you enjoy your visit to Tigger's Barn? I bet it was a bit frightening!'

'It was,' said George, truthfully, and said no more. He wanted to think about everything carefully, to sort out all he had heard, to try and piece together what had happened. It was all jumbled up in his mind.

One thing's certain, he thought, suddenly. We'll have to call a meeting of the Secret Seven. How strange that the Famous Five should have played a silly joke on us and led us to Something Big – another adventure, I'm sure. Susie's an idiot, but she's done the Secret Seven a very good turn!

As soon as George got home he felt in his pocket for the note that Zeb had given him. He felt round anxiously. It would have been dreadful if he had lost it!

But he hadn't. His fingers closed over the folded piece of paper. He took it out, his hand trembling with excitement. He opened it, and read it by the light of his bedroom lamp.

Dear Charlie,

Everything's ready and going OK. Can't see that anything can go wrong, but a fog would be very welcome as you can guess! Larry's looking after the points, we've arranged that. Don't forget the lorry, and get the tarpaulin truck cover marked with white at one corner. That'll save time in looking for the right load. It's clever of you to send out this load by truck, and collect it by lorry!

All the best,
Zeb

George couldn't make head or tail of this. What in the world was it all about? There was a plot of some kind, that was clear, but what did everything else mean?

George went to the telephone. Perhaps Peter wouldn't yet be in bed. He really MUST get on to him and tell him something important had happened.

Peter was just going to bed. He came to the telephone in surprise, when his mother called him to it.

'Hallo! What's up?'

'Peter, I can't stop to tell you everything now, but we went to Tigger's Barn, Jack and I, and there *is* something going on. We had quite an adventure, and—'

'You don't mean to tell me that that tale of Susie's was true!' said Peter, disbelievingly.

'No. At least, it was all made-up on her part, as you said, but all the same, something *is* going on at Tigger's Barn, Peter, something Susie didn't know about, of course, because she only mentioned the place in fun. But it's serious, Peter. You must call a meeting of the Secret Seven tomorrow evening after tea.'

There was a pause.

'Right,' said Peter, at last. 'I will. This is most odd, George. Don't tell me anything more over the phone, because I don't want Mother asking me too many questions. I'll tell Janet to tell Pam and Barbara there's a meeting tomorrow evening at five o'clock in our shed, and we'll tell Colin and Jack. Gosh! This sounds pretty mysterious.'

'You just wait till you hear the whole story!' said George. 'You'll be amazed.'

He put down the receiver, and got ready for bed, quite forgetting that he had had no supper. He couldn't stop thinking about the happenings of the evening. How odd that the password of the Secret Seven should be Cheeky Charlie, and there should be a real man called by that name!

And how extraordinary that Susie's bit of make-believe should suddenly have come true without her knowing it! Something *was* going on at Tigger's Barn!

He got into bed and lay awake for a long time. Jack was also lying awake thinking. He was excited. He wished he hadn't been shut up in that silly cupboard, when he might have been listening all the time. Still, George seemed to have got quite a lot of information.

The Secret Seven were very thrilled the next day. It was difficult not to let the Famous Five see that they had something exciting on hand, but Peter had strictly forbidden anyone to talk about the matter at school, just in *case* that tiresome Susie, with her long ears, got to hear of it.

'We don't want the Famous Five trailing us around,' said Peter. 'Just wait till this evening, all of you, and then we'll really get going!'

At five o'clock every single member of the Secret Seven was in the shed in Peter's garden. All of them had raced home quickly after afternoon school, gobbled their teas, and come rushing to the meeting.

The password was whispered quickly, as one after another passed into the shed, each wearing the badge with S.S. on. 'Cheeky Charlie, Cheeky Charlie, Cheeky Charlie.'

Jack and George had had little time to exchange more than a few words with one another. They were bursting to tell their strange story!

'Now, we're all here,' said Peter. 'Scamper, sit by the door and keep guard. Bark if you hear anything at all. This is a most important meeting.'

Scamper got up and went solemnly to the door. He sat down by it, listening, looking very serious.

'Oh, do hurry up, Peter,' said Pam. 'I can't wait a minute more to hear what it's all about!'

'All right, all right,' said Peter. 'You know that we weren't going to call another meeting till the Christmas hols, unless something urgent happened. Well, it's happened. Jack, you start off with the story, please.'

Jack was only too ready to tell it. He described how he had hidden in the laurel bush to overhear what the Famous Five said at their meeting in the summer-house. He repeated the ridiculous story that Susie had invented to deceive the Secret Seven, and to send them off on a wild-goose chase just to make fun of them.

He told them how Peter had laughed at the story and said it *was* just in Susie's imagination, but how he and George had decided to go to Tigger's Barn just in case it wasn't.

'But I was right,' interrupted Peter. 'It *was* a story, but just by chance there was some truth in it, too, though Susie didn't know.'

George took up the tale. He told the others how he and Jack had gone to Tigger's Barn, thinking that Susie and Jeff were in front of them. And then came the thrilling part of their adventure in the old tumbledown house!

Everyone listened intently, and held their breath when George came to the bit where the three men arrived.

Then Jack told how he went to the doorway to listen, and fell into the cupboard, and George told how he had gone to look for Jack, and had said the password, Cheeky Charlie, which had had such surprising results.

'Do you mean to say, there actually *is* a man called Cheeky Charlie?' asked Barbara, in amazement. 'Our password is only the name of a dog. Imagine there being a *man* called that, too! My goodness!'

'Don't interrupt,' said Peter. 'Go on, both of you.'

Everyone sat up with wide eyes when George told how the men had thought he was a messenger from Cheeky Charlie, and when he told them about the note they had given him, and produced it from his pocket, the Secret Seven were speechless with excitement!

The note was passed from hand to hand. Peter rapped on a box at last.

'We've all seen the note now,' he said. 'And we've heard Jack and George tell what happened last night. It's quite clear that we've hit on something strange again. Do the Secret Seven think we should try and solve this new mystery?'

Everyone yelled and banged on boxes, and Scamper barked in excitement too.

'Right,' said Peter. 'I agree too. But we have got to be very, very careful this time, or else the Famous Five will try and interfere, and they might spoil everything. Nobody – NOBODY – must say a single word about this to anyone in the world. Is that agreed?'

It was. Scamper came up and laid a big paw on Peter's knee, as if he thoroughly agreed too.

'Go back to the door, Scamper,' said Peter. 'We depend on you to give us warning if any of those tiresome Famous Five come snooping round. On guard, Scamper.'

Scamper trotted back to his place by the door obediently. The Seven crowded more closely together, and began a grand discussion.

'First, let's sort out all the things that Jack and George heard,' said Peter. 'Then we'll try and make out what they mean. At the moment I'm in a muddle about everything and haven't the slightest idea what the men are going to do.'

'Right,' said Jack. 'Well, as I told you, I heard the men talking, but their voices were very low, and I could only catch words now and again.'

'What words were they?' asked Peter. 'Tell us carefully.'

'Well, they kept saying something about "loading and unloading",' said Jack. 'And they kept on and on mentioning "points".'

'What sort of points?' asked Peter.

Jack shook his head, completely at a loss.

'I've no idea. They mentioned figures too. They said "six-two" quite a lot of times, and then they said "maybe seven-ten". And they said there mustn't be a moon, and I heard them talk about darkness, fog, and mist. Honestly, I couldn't make head or tail of it. I only know they must have been discussing some plan.'

'What else did you hear?' asked Janet.

'Nothing,' answered Jack. 'I fell into the cupboard then, and when the door shut on me I couldn't hear another word.'

'And all *I* can add is that the men asked me if Cheeky Charlie was at Dalling's or Hammond's,' said George. 'But goodness knows what *that* meant.'

'Perhaps they are the name of a workshop or works of some kind,' suggested Colin. 'We could find out.'

'Yes. We might be able to trace those,' said Peter. 'Now, this note. Whatever can it mean? It's got the word "points" here again. And they talk about trucks and lorries. It's plain that there's some robbery planned, I think. But what kind? They want fog, too. Well, that's understandable, I suppose.'

'Shall we take the note to the police?' said Barbara, suddenly gripped by a bright idea.

'Oh no! Not yet!' said George. 'It's *my*

note and I'd like to see if we can't do something about it ourselves before we tell any grown-ups. After all, we've managed lots of adventures very well so far. I don't see why we shouldn't be able to do something about this one too.'

'I'm all for trying,' said Peter. 'It's so exciting. And we've got quite a lot to go on, really. We know the names of three of the four men – Zeb, which is probably short for Zebedee, a most unusual name; and Larry, probably short for Laurence; and Cheeky Charlie, who is perhaps the boss.'

'Yes, and we know he's at Dalling's or Hammond's,' said Jack. 'What do we do first, Peter?'

Scamper suddenly began to bark wildly and scrape at the door.

'Not another word!' said Peter, sharply. 'There's someone outside!'

[11]

Any ideas?

Peter opened the door. Scamper tore out, barking. Then he stopped by a bush and wagged his tail. The Secret Seven ran to him.

A pair of feet showed at the bottom of the bush. Jack gave a shout of rage and pushed into the bush. He dragged someone out – Susie!

'How dare you!' he yelled. 'Coming here and listening! How dare you, Susie?'

'Let me go,' said Susie. 'I like you asking me how I dare! I'm only copying what *you* did on Saturday! Who hid in the laurel bush, and—'

'How did you know we were having a meeting?' demanded Jack, shaking Susie.

'I just followed you,' said Susie, grinning. 'But I didn't hear anything because I didn't dare to go near the door, in case Scamper barked. I did a sudden sneeze, though, and he must have heard me. What are you calling a meeting about?'

'As if we'd tell you!' said Peter, crossly. 'Go on home, Susie. Go on! Jack, take her home. The meeting is over.'

'Bother!' said Jack. 'All right. Come on, Susie. And if I have any nonsense from you, I'll pull your hair till you yell!'

Jack went off with Susie. Peter faced round to the others and spoke in a low voice.

'Listen. All of you think hard about what has been said, and give me or Janet any good ideas tomorrow. It's no good going on with this meeting. Somebody else belonging to the Famous Five might come snooping round too.'

'Right,' said the Secret Seven, and went

home, excited and very much puzzled. *How* could they think of anything that would help to piece together the jumble of words they knew? Points. Six-two, seven-ten. Fog, mist, darkness. Dalling's. Hammond's.

Each of them tried to think of some good idea. Barbara could think of nothing at all. Pam tried asking her father about Dalling's or Hammond's. He didn't know either of them. Pam felt awkward when he asked her why she wanted to know, and didn't go on with the subject.

Colin decided that a robbery was going to be done one dark and foggy night, and that the goods were to be unloaded from a lorry somewhere. He couldn't imagine why they were to be sent in a truck. All the boys thought exactly the same thing, but, as Peter said, it wasn't much help because they didn't know what date, what place, or what lorry!

Then Jack had quite a good idea. He

thought it would be helpful if they tried to find a man called Zebedee, because surely he must be the Zeb at Tigger's Barn. There couldn't be *many* Zebedees in the district!

'All right, Jack. It's a good *idea*,' said Peter. 'You can do the finding out for us. Produce this Zeb, and that may be the first step.'

'Yes, but how shall I find out?' said Jack. 'I can't go round asking every man I meet if he's called Zeb.'

'No. That's why I said it was a good *idea*,' said Peter, grinning. 'But that's about all it is. It's an impossible thing to do, you see; so that's why it will remain just a good idea and nothing else. Finding the only Zebedee in the district would be like looking for a needle in a haystack.'

'I shouldn't like to have to do *that*,' said Janet, who was with them. 'Peter and I have got about the only good idea, I think, Jack.'

'What's that?' asked Jack.

'Well, we looked in our telephone directory at home to see if any firm called Dalling or Hammond was there,' said Janet. 'But there wasn't, so we thought they must be somewhere farther off, not in our district at all. Our telephone book only gives the names of people in this area, you see.'

'And now we're going to the post office to look in the big telephone directories there,' said Peter. 'They give the names of districts much farther away. Like to come with us?'

Jack went with them. They came to the post office and went in. Peter took up two telephone books, one with the Ds in and one with the Hs.

'Now I'll look for Dalling,' he said, and thumbed through the Ds. The other two leaned over him, looking down the Ds too.

'Dale, Dale, Dale, Dales, Dalgleish, Daling, Dalish, Dallas, DALLING!' read Peter, his finger following down the list of names. 'Here it is – Dalling. Oh, there are three Dallings! Bother!'

'There's a Mrs A. Dalling, Rose Cottage, Hubley,' said Janet. 'And E.A. Dalling, of Manor House, Tallington, and Messrs. E. Dalling, Manufacturers of Lead Goods. Well – which would be the right Dalling? The manufacturers, I suppose.'

'Yes,' said Peter, sounding excited. 'Now for the Hs. Where are they? In the other book. Here we are – Hall, Hall – goodness, what a lot of people are called Hall! Hallet, Ham, Hamm, Hammers, Hamming, Hammond, Hammond, Hammond, Hammond – oh, LOOK!'

They all looked. Peter was pointing to the fourth name of Hammond. 'Hammond and Co. Ltd. Lead Manufacturers, Petlington.'

'There you are,' said Peter, triumphantly. 'Two firms dealing in lead, one called

Hammond, one called Dalling. Cheeky Charlie must be something to do with both.'

'Lead!' said Jack. 'It's very valuable nowadays, isn't it? I'm always reading about thieves going and stealing it off church roofs. I don't know why churches so often have lead roofs, but they seem to.'

'It looks as if Cheeky Charlie might be going to send a load of lead off somewhere in a truck, and Zeb and the others are going to stop it, and take the lead,' said Peter. 'As you say, it's very valuable, Jack.'

'Charlie must have quite a high position if he's in both firms,' said Janet. 'Oh, dear – I do wonder what his real name is! Cheeky Charlie! I wonder why they call him that?'

'Because he's bold and has got plenty of cheek, I expect,' said Peter. 'If only Hammond's and Dalling's weren't so far away! We could go and snoop round there and see if we could hear of anyone called Cheeky Charlie.'

'They're miles away,' said Jack, looking at the addresses. 'Well, we've been quite clever, but I don't see that we've got very much farther, really. We just know that Dalling's and Hammond's are firms that deal in lead, which is very valuable stuff, but that's all!'

'Yes. It doesn't take us very far,' said Peter, shutting up the directory. 'We'll have to think a bit harder. Come on, let's go and buy some sweets. Sucking a bit of toffee always seems to help my thinking!'

[12]

A game – and a brainwave!

Another day went by, and Saturday came. A meeting was called for that morning, but nobody had much to say. In fact, it was rather a dull meeting after the excitement of the last one. The Seven sat in the shed eating biscuits provided by Jack's mother, and Scamper was at the door, on guard as usual.

It was raining outside. The Seven looked out dismally.

'No good going for a walk, or having a game of football,' said Peter. 'Let's stay here in the shed and play a game.'

'Fetch your railway set, Peter,' said Janet. 'And I'll fetch the farm set. We could set out the lines here in the middle of the toy trees and farm buildings, looking as if they were real countryside. We've got heaps of farm stuff.'

'Oh yes. Let's do that,' said Pam. 'I love your farm set. It's the nicest and biggest I've ever seen. Do get it! We could set it out, and then we could put up the railway.'

'It's a jolly good thing to do on a rainy morning like this,' said Jack, pleased. 'I wanted to help Jeff with *his* brilliant railway the other day, when George came to tea with me, but he was Susie's guest, and she wouldn't have let us join in for anything. You know, she's very suspicious that we're working on something, Peter. She keeps on and on at me to tell her if anything happened at Tigger's Barn that night.'

'Well, just shut her up,' said Peter. 'Scamper, you needn't watch the door any more. You can come and join us, old fellow. The meeting's over.'

Scamper was pleased. He ran round everyone, wagging his tail. Peter fetched his railway set, and Janet and Pam went to get the big farm set. It had absolutely everything, from animals and farm men to trees, fences, troughs and sties!

They all began to put up the two sets – putting together the lines and setting out a proper little countryside, with trees, fences, animals and farm buildings. It really was fun.

Peter suddenly looked up at the window. He had noticed a movement there. He saw a face looking in, and leapt up with such a fierce yell that everyone jumped in alarm.

'It's Jeff,' he cried. 'I wonder if he's snooping round for the Famous Five. After him, Scamper!'

But Jeff had taken to his heels, and, even if Scamper had caught him, nothing would have happened, because the spaniel knew Jeff well and liked him.

'It doesn't really matter Jeff looking in,' said Janet. 'All he'd see would be us having a very peaceful game! Let him stand out in the rain and look in if he wants to!'

The railway lines were ready at last. The three beautiful clockwork engines were attached to their line of trucks. Two were passenger trains and one was a goods train.

'I'll manage one train, you can do another train, Colin, and you can have a third one, Jack,' said Peter. 'Janet, you do the signals. You're good at those. And, George, you work the points. We mustn't have an accident. You can always switch one of the trains on to another line, if two look like crashing.'

'Right. I'll manage the points,' said George, pleased. 'I like doing those. I love seeing a train being switched off a main-line into a siding.'

The engines were wound up and set going. They tore round the floor, and George switched them cleverly from one line to another when it seemed there might be an accident.

And, in the middle of all this, Janet suddenly sat up straight, and said in a loud voice: 'WELL, I NEVER!'

The others looked at her.

'What's the matter?' said Peter. 'Well, I never *what*? Why are you looking as if you are going to burst?'

'Points!' said Janet, excitedly. 'Points!' And she waved her hand to where George was sitting working the points, switching the trains from one line to another. 'Oh, Peter, don't be so *stupid*! Don't you remember? Those men at Tigger's Barn talked about *points*. Jack said they kept *on* mentioning them. Well, I bet they were *points on some railway line*!'

There was a short silence. Then everyone spoke at once. 'Yes! It could be! Why didn't we think of it before? Of course! Points on the railway!'

The game stopped at once and an eager discussion began.

'Why should they use the points? It must be because they want to switch a train on to another line.'

'Yes, a train that contains something they want to steal – lead, probably!'

'Then it's a goods train. One of the trucks must be carrying the lead they want to steal!'

'The tarpaulin! Would that be covering up the load? Don't you remember? It had to be marked with white at the corner, so that the men would know it.'

'Yes! They wouldn't have to waste time then looking into every truck to see which was the right one. Sometimes there are thirty or forty trucks on a goods train. The white marks on the tarpaulin would tell them at once they had the right truck!'

'Woof,' said Scamper, joining in the general excitement.

Peter turned to him. 'Hey, Scamper, on guard at the door again, old fellow!' he said, at once. 'The meeting's begun again! On guard!'

Scamper went on guard. The Secret Seven drew close together, suddenly very excited. To think that one simple word had set their brains working like this, and put them on the right track at once!

'You are really clever, Janet,' said Jack, and Janet beamed.

'Oh, anyone might have thought of it,' she said. 'It just rang a bell in my mind somehow, when you kept saying "points". Oh, Peter, where are these points, do you think?'

Peter was following out another idea in his mind. 'I've thought of something else,' he said, his eyes shining. 'Those figures the men kept saying. Six-two, seven-ten. Couldn't they be the times of trains?'

'Oh *yes*! Like when we say Daddy's going to catch the six-twenty home, or the seven-twelve!' cried Pam. 'Six-two – there must be a train that starts somewhere at six-two. Or arrives somewhere then.'

'And they want a foggy or misty, dark night, because then it would be easy to switch the train into some siding,' said Jack. 'A foggy night would be marvellous for them. The engine-driver couldn't possibly see that his train had been switched off on the wrong line. He'd go on till he came to some signal, and the men would be there ready to take the lead from the marked truck . . .'

'And they'd deal with the surprised engine-driver, and the guard too, I suppose,' said Colin.

There was a silence after this. It suddenly dawned on the Seven that there must be quite a big gang engaged in this particular robbery.

'I think we ought to tell somebody,' said Pam.

Peter shook his head. 'No. Let's find out

more if we can. And I'm sure we can now! For instance, let's get a timetable and see if there's a train that arrives anywhere at two minutes past six – six–two.'

'That's no good,' said Jack, at once. 'Goods trains aren't in the timetables.'

'Oh no. I forgot that,' said Peter. 'Well, what about one or two of us going down to the station and asking a few questions about goods trains and what time they come in, and where from? We know where the firms of Dalling and Hammond are. Where was it now – Petlington, wasn't it?'

'Yes,' said Janet. 'That's a good idea of yours to go down to the station, Peter. It's stopped raining. Why don't you go now?'

'I will,' said Peter. 'You come with me, Colin. Jack and George have had plenty of excitement so far, but you haven't had very much. Come on down to the station with me.'

So off went the two boys, looking rather thrilled. They really were on the trail now!

Peter and Colin arrived at the station just as a train was coming in. They watched it. Two porters were on the platform, and a man stood with them in dirty blue overalls. He had been working on the line, and had hopped up on to the platform when the train came rumbling in.

The boys waited till the train had gone out. Then they went up to one of the porters.

'Are there any goods trains coming through?' asked Peter. 'We like watching them.'

'There's one in fifteen minutes' time,' said the porter.

'Is it a very long one?' said Colin. 'I once counted forty-seven trucks pulled by a goods engine.'

'The longest one comes in here in the evening,' said the porter. 'How many trucks do you reckon it has as a rule, Zeb?'

The man in dirty overalls rubbed a black hand over his face, and pushed back his cap. 'Well, maybe thirty, maybe forty. It depends.'

The boys looked at one another. *Zeb*! The porter had called the linesman *Zeb*! Could it be – could it *possibly* be the same Zeb that had met the other two men at Tigger's Barn?

They looked at him. He wasn't much to look at, certainly, a thin, mean-faced little man, very dirty, and with hair much too long. Zeb! It was such an unusual name that the boys felt sure they must be face to face with the Zeb who had been up at the old tumbledown house.

'Er – what time does this goods train come in the evening?' asked Peter, finding his tongue again at last.

'It comes in about six o'clock twice a week,' said Zeb. 'Six-two, it's supposed to be here, but sometimes it's late.'

'Where does it come from?' asked Colin.

'Plenty of places!' said Zeb, 'Turleigh, Idlesston, Hayley, Garton, Petlington . . .'

'Petlington!' said Colin, before he could stop himself. That was the place where the firms of Dalling and Hammond were. Peter scowled at him, and Colin hurried to cover up his mistake in calling attention to the town they were so interested in.

'Petlington, yes, go on, where else?' said Colin.

The linesman gave him another string of names, and the boys listened. But they had learnt already a good deal of what they wanted to know.

The six–two was a goods train, that came in twice a week, and Petlington was one of the places it came from, probably with a truck or two added there, full of lead goods from Hammond's and Dalling's! Lead pipes? Sheets of lead? The boys had no idea, and it didn't really matter. It was lead, anyway, valuable lead, they were sure of that! Lead sent off by Cheeky Charlie for his firms.

'We've been playing with my model railway this morning,' said Peter, suddenly thinking of a way to ask about points and switches. 'It's a really good one, it's got points to switch my trains from one line to another. Very good they are too, as good as real points!'

'Ah, you want to ask my mate about *them*,' said Zeb. 'He's got plenty to deal with. He uses them to switch the goods trains from one part of the line to another. They often have to go into sidings, you know.'

'Does he switch the six–two into a siding?' said Peter. 'Or does it go straight through on the main-line?'

'Straight through,' said Zeb. 'No, Larry only switches the goods trains that have to be unloaded near here. The six–two goes right on to Swindon. You'll see it this evening if you come down.'

Peter had given a quick look at Colin to see if he had noticed the name of Zeb's mate – Larry! Zeb and Larry – what an enormous piece of luck! Colin gave a quick wink at Peter. Yes, he had noticed all right! He began to look excited.

'I wish we could see Larry working the points,' said Peter. 'It must be fun. I expect the switches are quite different from the ones on my railway lines at home.'

Zeb laughed. 'You bet they are! Ours take some moving! Look, would you like to walk along the line with me, and I'll show you some switches that send a train off into a siding? It's about a mile up the line.'

Peter took a look at his watch. He would be very late for his dinner, but this was really important. Why, he might see the very points that Larry was going to use one dark, foggy night!

'Look out the kids don't get knocked down by a train,' the porter warned Zeb, as the linesman took the two boys down on to the track with him.

The boys looked at him with scorn. As if they couldn't tell when a train was coming!

It seemed a very long way up the line. Zeb had a job of work not far from the points. He left his tools by the side of the line he was to repair, and took the boys to where a number of lines crossed one another. He explained how the points worked.

'You pull this lever for that line, see? Watch how the rails move so that they lead to that other line over there, instead of letting the train keep on this line.'

Colin and Peter did a little pulling of levers themselves, and they found it exceptionally hard work.

'Does the six–two come on this line?' asked Peter, innocently.

'Yes. But it goes straight on; it doesn't get

switched to one side,' said Zeb. 'It never has goods for this district; it goes on to Swindon. Now don't you ever mess about on the railway by yourselves, or the police will be after you straight away!'

'We won't,' promised the two boys.

'Well, I must get on with my job,' said Zeb, not sounding as if he wanted to at all. 'So long! Hope I've told you what you wanted to know.'

He certainly had, much, much more than he imagined. Colin and Peter could hardly believe their luck. They made their way to the side of the line, and stood there for a while.

'We ought really to go and explore the siding,' said Peter. 'But we're dreadfully late. Bother! We forgot to ask what evenings the goods train comes in from Petlington!'

'Let's get back, and come again this afternoon,' said Colin. 'I'm so hungry. We can find out the two days the goods train comes through when we're here this afternoon, and explore the siding too.'

They left the railway and went to the road. They were both so excited that they could hardly stop talking. 'Fancy bumping into Zeb! Zeb himself! And hearing about Larry in charge of the points! Why, everything's as plain as can be. What a good thing Janet had the brain-wave this morning about points! My goodness, we are in luck!'

'We'll be back this afternoon as soon as we can,' said Peter. 'I vote the whole lot of us go. Gosh, this *is* getting exciting!'

[13]

An exciting afternoon

Both Peter's mother and Colin's were very angry when they arrived back so late for their dinner. Janet was so full of curiosity to know what had happened that she could hardly wait till Peter had finished. He kept frowning at her as he gobbled down his hot stew, afraid that she would ask some awkward questions.

He sent her round to collect the Secret Seven, and they all arrived in a very short time, though Colin was late because he had to finish his dinner.

Peter told them everything, and they listened, thrilled. Well, what a tale! To meet Zeb like that, and to have him telling them so much that they wanted to know!

'Little did he know why we asked him so many questions!' said Colin, with a grin. 'I must say he was quite nice to us, though he's a mean-looking man with shifty eyes.'

'This afternoon we will all go to the siding,' said Peter. 'We'll find out what days that goods train comes along, too.'

So off they went. First they went to the station and found the porter again. He had nothing much to do and was pleased to talk to them. He told them tales of this, that and the other on the railway, and gradually Peter guided him to the subject of goods trains.

'Here comes one,' said the porter. 'It won't stop at the station, though – no passengers to get on or off, you see. Want to count the trucks? It's not a very long train.'

Most of the trucks were open ones, and they carried all kinds of things, coal, bricks, machinery, crates. The train rumbled by slowly, and the Seven counted thirty-two trucks.

'I'd rather like to see that goods train Zeb told us about,' said Peter to the porter. 'The one that comes from Petlington and beyond, the six–two, I think he said. It's sometimes a very long one, isn't it?'

'Yes. Well, you'd have to come on Tuesday or Friday,' said the porter. 'But it's dark then, so you won't see much. Look, the guard of that last goods train is waving to you!'

They waved back. The goods train got smaller and smaller in the distance and at last disappeared.

'I wonder things aren't stolen out of those open trucks,' said Peter, innocently.

'Oh, they are,' said the porter. 'There's been a whole lot of stealing lately, yes, even a car taken out of one truck, though you mightn't believe it! Some gang at work, they say. Beats me how they do it! Well, you kids, I must go and do a spot of work. So long!'

The Seven wandered off. They walked by the side of the track for about a mile until they came to where the points were that Zeb had explained that morning.

Peter pointed them out. 'That's where they plan to switch the goods train off to a side-line,' he said. 'I wish we knew which evening. I think it must be soon, though, because that note George got said that everything was ready and going OK.'

They followed the side-line, walking by the side of the railway. The line meandered off all by itself and finally came into a little goods yard, which seemed to be completely deserted at that moment.

Big gates led into the goods yard. They were open to let in lorries that came to take the goods unloaded from trucks sent down the side-line. But only empty trucks stood on the little line now, and not a soul was about. It was plain that no goods train was expected for some time.

'This is a very lonely little place,' said Colin. 'If a goods train was diverted down here, nobody would hear it or see it, except those who would be waiting for it! I bet there will be a lorry creeping in here some evening, ready to take the lead sheets or pipes or whatever they are, from the truck whose tarpaulin is marked with white lines!'

'What about coming here on Tuesday evening, just in *case* that's the night they've arranged?' said Jack, suddenly. 'Then, if we saw anything happening, we could telephone the police. And before Zeb and Larry and the other two could finish their unloading we could get the police here. I say, wouldn't that be a thrill?'

'I don't know. I think really we ought to get in touch with that big Inspector we like,' said Peter. 'We know quite enough now to be sure of what we say. The only thing we *don't* know is whether it's this Tuesday or if it's to be later on.'

They stood together, arguing, and nobody saw a burly policeman sauntering in through the open gates. He stared when he saw the children, and stood watching them.

'I'd like to see those points,' said Colin, getting tired of the argument. 'Show me them, Peter. We'll look out for trains.'

Peter forgot that children were not allowed to trespass on the railway lines. He set off up the side-line with the others, walking in the middle of the lines on his way to the points.

A loud voice hailed them. 'Hey, you kids there! What do you think you're doing, trespassing like that? You come back here. I've got something to say to you.'

'Let's run!' said Pam, in a panic. 'Don't let him catch us.'

'No. We can't run,' said Peter. 'I forgot

we ought not to walk on the lines like this. Come back and explain, and if we say we're sorry, we'll be all right!'

So he led all the Seven back into the goods yard. The policeman came up to them, frowning.

'Now you look here,' he said; 'there's been too much nonsense from children on the railways lately. I've a good mind to take all your names and addresses and make a complaint to your parents about you.'

'But we weren't doing a thing!' said Peter, indignantly. 'We're sorry we trespassed, but honestly we weren't doing a scrap of harm.'

'What are you doing in this here goods yard?' said the policeman. 'Up to some mischief, no doubt!'

'We're not,' said Peter.

'Well, what did you come here for, then?' said the policeman. 'Go on, tell me. You didn't come here for nothing.'

'Tell him,' said Barbara, frightened and almost crying.

The policeman became very suspicious at once when he heard that there was something to tell. 'Oho! So there *was* something you were after!' he said. 'Now you just tell me, or I'll take your names and addresses!'

Peter wasn't going to tell this bad-tempered man anything. For one thing, he wouldn't believe the extraordinary tale that the Secret Seven had to tell, and for another, Peter wasn't going to give all his secrets away! No, if he was going to tell anyone, he would tell his father, or the Inspector they all liked so much!

It ended in the big policeman losing his temper thoroughly and taking down all their names and addresses, one by one. It was really maddening. To think they had come there to help to catch a gang of clever thieves, and had had their names taken for trespassing!

'I'll get told off if my father hears about this,' said Colin, dolefully. 'Oh, Peter, let's tell our nice Inspector everything, before that policeman goes round to our parents.'

But Peter was angry and obstinate. 'No!' he said. 'We'll settle this affair ourselves, and the police can come in at the last moment, when we've done everything, yes, that horrid man, too, who took our names. Think of his face if he has to come along to this goods yard one night to catch thieves *we've* tracked down, instead of him! I'll feel jolly pleased to crow over him!'

'I'd like to come, too, on that night,' said Janet.

'Well I think just a few of us should go. If things turn dangerous it'll be better if there's just four of us rather than seven!'

No one could argue with that, so they decided that Jack, Colin, George and Peter should go alone.

[14]

Tuesday evening at last!

There was a meeting the next morning to talk over everything and to make arrangements for Tuesday. It was a proper November day, and a mist hung everywhere.

'My father says there will be a fog before tomorrow,' announced Peter. 'If so those men are going to be lucky on Tuesday. I don't expect the driver of the engine will even guess his train's on the side-line when the points send him there! He won't be able to see a thing.'

'I wish Tuesday would buck up and come,' said Jack. 'Susie *knows* there's something up, and she and her Famous Five are just *longing* to know what it is! Won't she be wild when she knows that it was her silly trick that put us on to all this?'

'Yes. I guess that will be the end of the Famous Five,' said Colin. 'Hey, Peter, look here. I managed to get hold of a railway map. My father had one. It shows the lines from Petlington, and all the points and everything. Jack, do you think it could have been a map like this that Zeb and Larry and the other man were looking at in Tigger's Barn?'

'Yes. It may have been,' said Jack. 'I bet those men have played this kind of game before. They know the railway so well. Oh, I do wish Tuesday would come!'

Tuesday did come at last. Not one of the Secret Seven could do good work at school that day. They kept on and on thinking of the coming night. Peter looked out of the window a hundred times that morning!

Dad was right, he thought. The fog did come down, a real November fog. And tonight it will be so thick that there will be fog-signals on the railways. We shall hear them go off.

The four boys had arranged to meet after tea, with Scamper. Peter thought it would be a good thing to take him with them in case anything went wrong.

They all had torches. Peter felt to see if he had any sweets in his pocket to share with his friends. He had! Jolly good! He shivered with excitement.

He nearly didn't go with the others, because his mother saw him putting his coat on, and was horrified to think that he was going out into the fog.

'You'll get lost,' she said. 'You mustn't go.'

'I'm meeting the others,' said Peter, desperately. 'I *must* go.'

'I really can't let you,' said his mother. 'Well – not unless you take Scamper with you. He'll know the way home if you don't!'

'Oh, I'm taking Scamper, of *course*,' said Peter thankfully, and escaped at once, Scamper at his heels. He met the others at his gate and they set off.

The thick fog swirled round them, and their torches could hardly pierce it. Then they heard the bang-bang of the fog-signals on the railway.

'I bet Zeb and the rest are pleased with this fog!' said Colin. 'Look, there's the fence that runs beside the railway. If we keep close to that we can't lose our way.'

They arrived at the goods yard about five minutes to six, and went cautiously in at the gates, which were open. All the boys had rubber-soled shoes on, and they carefully switched off their torches as they went quietly into the goods yard.

They heard the sound of a lorry's engine throbbing, and stopped. Voices came to them, low voices, and then they saw a lantern held by someone.

'The gang are here, and the lorry sent by Cheeky Charlie!' whispered Jack. 'You can just see it over there. I bet it's got the name of Hammond or Dalling on it!'

'It *was* this Tuesday,' said Colin, in relief. 'I did hope we hadn't come all the way here in this fog for nothing.'

Bang! Bang-bang!

More fog-signals went off and yet more. The boys knew when trains were running over the main-line some distance away because of the sudden explosions of the fog-signals, warning the drivers to look out for the real signals or to go slowly.

'What's the time?' whispered George.

'It's about half-past six now,' whispered back Peter. 'The six–two is late because of the fog. It may be along any time now, or it may be very late, of course.'

BANG! Another fog-signal went off in the next few minutes. The boys wondered if it had gone off under the wheels of the late goods train.

It had. The driver put his head out of his train and looked for the signal. It shone green. He could go on. He went on slowly, not knowing he was on the wrong line! Larry was there at the points, well-hidden by the darkness and the fog, and he had switched the goods train carefully on to the little side-line!

The goods train left the main-line. It would not go through the station tonight, it would only go into the little goods yard, where silent men awaited it. Larry switched the levers again, so that the next train would go safely on to the main-line. He did not want half a dozen trains on the side-line together! Then he ran down the single-line after the slow-moving train.

'It's coming! I can hear it,' whispered Peter suddenly, and he caught hold of Jack's arm. 'Let's go over there by that shed. We can see everything without being seen. Come on!'

Rumble-rumble-rumble! The goods train came nearer. The red eye of a lamp gleamed in the fog. Now what was going to happen?

[15]

In the goods yard

A fog-signal went off just where the gang wanted the train to stop. Bang!

The engine pulled up at once, and the trucks behind clang-clanged as they bumped into one another. A hurried talk had gone on between Zeb, Larry and four other men by the coach. The boys could hear every word.

'We'll tell him he's on the wrong line. We'll pretend to be surprised to see him there. Larry, you tell him he'd better stay on this side-line till the fog clears and he can get orders and go back. Take him off to that shed and hot up some tea or something. Keep him there while we do the job!'

The others nodded.

Peter whispered to Jack: 'They're going to tell the engine-driver that he's run off the main-line by mistake into this side-line, and then take him off out of the way, the guard too, I expect. There won't be any fighting, which is a good thing.'

'Sh!' said Jack. 'Look, the engine-driver is jumping down. He's lost, I expect! Doesn't know where he is!'

'Hey, there, engine-driver, you're on the side-line!' called Larry's voice, and he ran up to the engine, a lamp swaying in his hands. 'You ought to be on the main-line, running through the station.'

'Ay, I should be,' said the driver, puzzled. 'There must have been some mistake at the points. Am I safe here, mate?'

'Safe as can be!' called back Larry, cheerily. 'Don't you worry! You're in a goods yard, well out of the way of main-line traffic. Better not move till you get orders, this fog's terrible!'

'Good thing I got on to a side-line, that's all I can say,' said the driver. The guard came up at that moment from the last van, and joined in the conversation. He thought it peculiar.

'Someone making a mess of the points,' he grumbled. 'Now we'll be here for the night, and my missus is expecting me for supper.'

'Well, you may be home for breakfast if the fog clears,' said the driver, comfortingly.

The guard didn't think so. He was very gloomy.

'Well, mates, come along to this shed,' said Larry. 'There's an oil-stove there, and we'll light up and have a cup of something hot. Don't worry about telephoning for orders. I'll do all that.'

'Who are you?' asked the gloomy guard.

'Who, me? I'm in charge of this yard,' said Larry, most untruthfully. 'Don't you worry now. It's a blessing you got on to this side-line. I bet your orders will be to stay here for the night. I'll have to find somewhere for you to settle down.'

They all disappeared into the shed. A glow soon came from the window. Peter daringly peeped in, and saw the three men round an oil-stove, and a kettle on top to boil water for tea.

Then things moved remarkably quickly. Zeb disappeared down the side-line to look for the truck covered by the tarpaulin with white marks. It was the seventh one, as he informed the others when he came back.

'We'll start up the lorry, and take it to the truck,' he said. 'Fortunately it's just where the yard begins, so we shan't have to carry the stuff far. Good thing, too, because it's heavy.'

The lorry was started up, and ran cautiously up the yard to the far end. There it stopped, presumably by the seventh truck. The four boys went silently through the fog and watched what happened for a minute or two.

The men were untying the tarpaulin by the light of a railway lantern. Soon it was entirely off. Jack could see the white paint at one corner that had marked it for the men.

Then began a pulling and tugging and panting as the men hauled up the goods inside. What were they? The boys couldn't see.

'Sheets of lead, I think,' whispered Colin. 'Peter, when are we going to telephone the police? Don't you think we'd better do that now?'

'Yes,' whispered back Peter. 'Come on. There's a telephone in that little brick building over there. I noticed telephone wires going to the chimney there this afternoon. One of the windows is a bit open. We'll get in there. Where's Scamper? Oh, there you are. Now, not a sound, old boy!'

Scamper had behaved perfectly. Not a

bark, not a whine had come from him, though he was very puzzled by the evening's happenings. He trotted at Peter's heels as the four boys went to telephone.

They had to pass the lorry on the way. Peter stopped dead and listened. No one was in the lorry. The men were still unloading the truck.

To the astonishment of the other three, he left them, leapt up into the driving seat and down again.

'Whatever are you doing?' whispered Jack.

'I took the key that turns on the engine!' said Peter, excited. 'Now they can't drive the lorry away!'

'Gosh!' said the others, lost in admiration at Peter's quickness. 'You *are* smart, Peter!'

They went to the little stone building. The door was locked, but, as Peter said, a window was open just a little. It was easy to force it up. In went Peter and flashed his torch round quickly to find the telephone. Ah yes, there it was. Good!

He switched off his torch and picked up the receiver. He heard the operator's voice.

'Number, please?'

'Police station – quickly!' said Peter.

And in two seconds a voice came again. 'Police station here.'

'Is the Inspector there, please?' asked Peter, urgently. 'Please tell him it's Peter, and I want to speak to him quickly.'

This peculiar message was passed on to the Inspector, who happened to be in the room. He came to the telephone at once.

'Yes, yes? Peter who? Oh *you*, Peter! What's up?'

Peter told him. 'Sir, I can't tell you all the details now, but the six–two goods train has been switched off the main-line on to the side-line here, near Kepley, where there's a goods yard. And there is a gang of men unloading lead from one of the waggons into a lorry nearby. I think a man called Cheeky Charlie is in charge of things, sir.'

'Cheeky Charlie! Chee— How do *you* know anything about that fellow?' cried the Inspector, filled with amazement. 'All right, don't waste time telling me now. I'll send men out straight away. Look out for them, and look out for yourselves too. That gang is dangerous. Cheeky Charlie, well, my word!'

[16]

Hurrah for the Secret Seven!

It seemed a long time before any police cars came. The four boys were so excited that they could not keep still. Peter felt as if he really must go and see how the gang was getting on.

He crept out into the yard, and made his way to the lorry. It was dark there, and quiet. He crept forward, and suddenly bumped into someone standing still beside it.

The someone gave a shout and caught him. 'Here, who's this? What are you doing?'

Then a light was flashed on him, and Zeb's voice said: 'You! The kid who was asking questions the other day! What are you up to?'

He shook Peter so roughly that the boy almost fell over. And then Scamper came flying up!

'Grrrrrrrr!' He flew at Zeb and nipped him sharply on the leg. Zeb gave a yell. Two of the other men came running up. 'What's the matter? What's up?'

'A boy – and a dog!' growled Zeb. 'We'd better get going. Is the unloading finished? That kid may give the alarm.'

'Where is he? Why didn't you hang on to him?' said one of the men, angrily.

'The dog bit me, and I had to let the boy go,' said Zeb, rubbing his leg. 'They've both disappeared into the fog. Come on, hurry, I've got the wind up now.'

Peter had shot back to the others, alarmed at being so nearly caught. He bent down and fondled Scamper. 'Good boy!' he whispered. 'Brave dog! Well done, Scamper!'

Scamper wagged his tail, pleased. He

didn't understand in the least why Peter should have brought him to this peculiar place in a thick fog, but he was quite happy to be with him anywhere.

'When's that police car coming?' whispered Colin, shivering as much with excitement as with cold.

'Soon, I expect,' whispered back Peter. 'Ah, here it comes – no, two of them!'

The sound of cars coming down the road that led to the goods yards was plainly to be heard. They came slowly, because of the fog. They would have got there very much more quickly if the evening had been clear.

They came into the yard and stopped. Peter ran to the first one. It was driven by the Inspector, and had four policemen in it. The second car was close behind, and policemen in plain clothes tumbled swiftly out of it.

'Sir! You've come just in time!' said Peter. 'Their lorry is over there. They've loaded it now. You'll catch them just at the right moment!'

The police ran over to the dark shape in the fog, the big lorry. Zeb, Larry, Cheeky Charlie and the other men were all in it, with the load of lead behind, but try as Zeb would he could not find the starting-key of the lorry!

'Start her up quickly, you ninny!' said Cheeky Charlie. 'The police are here! Drive the lorry at them if they try to stop us!'

'The key's gone. It must have dropped down,' wailed Zeb, and flashed a torch on to the floor below the steering-wheel. But it was not a bit of good looking there, of course. It was safely in Peter's pocket!

The police closed round the silent lorry. 'Game's up, Charlie,' said the Inspector's stern voice. 'You coming quietly, or not? We've got you right on the spot!'

'You wouldn't have, if we could have got this lorry to move!' shouted Zeb, angrily.

'Who's got the key? That's what I want to know. Who's got it?'

'I have,' called Peter. 'I took it out myself so that you couldn't get away in the lorry!'

'Good boy! Smart lad!' said a nearby policeman, admiringly, and gave the delighted Peter a thump on the back.

The fog suddenly thinned, and the scene became clearer in the light of many torches and lamps. The engine-driver and the guard came out of the shed in amazement, wondering what was happening. They had been left comfortably there by Zeb, drinking tea and playing cards.

The gang made no fuss. It wasn't worth it, with so many strong men around! They were bundled into the police cars, which drove away at a faster speed than they had come, thanks to the thinning of the fog!

'I'll walk back with you,' said the Inspector's cheerful voice. 'There's no room in the cars for me now. There's a bit of a squash there at the moment!'

He told the engine-driver to report what had happened to his headquarters by telephone, and left the astonished man, and the equally astonished fireman and guard, to look after themselves and their train.

Then he and the four boys trudged back to Peter's house. How amazed his mother was when she opened the door and found four of them with the big Inspector!

'Oh dear, what have they been up to now?' she said. 'A policeman has just been round complaining about Peter trespassing on the railway the other day, with his friends. Oh, don't say he's done anything terribly wrong!'

'Well, he's certainly been trespassing on the railway again,' said the Inspector, with a broad smile, 'but what he's done this time is terribly right, not terribly wrong. Let me come in and tell you.'

So, with a very excited Janet listening, the tale of that evening was told.

'And, you see,' finished the Inspector, 'we've got our hands on Cheeky Charlie at last. He's the boss of this gang that robs the goods trucks all over the place. A clever fellow but not *quite* so clever as the Secret Seven!'

The Inspector left at last, beaming, full of admiration once more for the Secret Seven. Peter turned to the others.

'Tomorrow,' he said solemnly, but with his face glowing – 'tomorrow we call a meeting of the Secret Seven – and we ask the Famous Five to come along too!'

'But why?' said Janet, surprised.

'Just so that we can tell them how the Secret Seven manage their affairs!' said Peter. 'And to thank them for putting us on the track of this most exciting adventure!'

'Ha! Susie won't like that!' said Jack.

'She certainly won't,' said Janet. 'Famous Five indeed! This will be the end of *them*!'

'Up with the Secret Seven!' said Jack, grinning. 'Hurrah for us – hip-hip-hurrah!'

GO AHEAD, SECRET SEVEN

[1]

Susie is most annoying

Peter was going home from school one afternoon, swinging his satchel, when someone came running behind him and bumped into him.

He dropped his bag and almost fell over. He looked round crossly, expecting it to be George or Colin. But it wasn't. It was Susie with her cheeky face, standing by the kerb grinning at him.

'Sorry!' she said. 'You were in my way. How's the Secret Seven Society going?'

'You just look where you're going, Susie,' said Peter, picking up his bag. 'As for the Secret Seven, it's no business of *yours*. You're always trying to interfere!'

'Jack says there haven't been any Secret

Seven meetings for ages,' said Susie, walking beside Peter, much to his annoyance. Susie was the most aggravating girl he knew.

Jack was Susie's brother, and a member of the Secret Seven. Peter was quite sure he hadn't said anything about the meetings. But Susie was right. They hadn't had any meetings for a long time. The Easter term had been rather exciting so far, and Peter hadn't thought a great deal about his Secret Society.

'Well, we're having a Secret Seven meeting very soon,' he said to Susie, making up his mind suddenly that they would. 'But you're not coming! And if you try any silly snooping, you'll be sorry. You don't belong to our Society, and you never will.'

'I know your last password,' said Susie, skipping over the cracks in the paving-stones. 'Aha!'

'You don't,' said Peter, racking his brains

to remember what it was. Goodness – it wouldn't do for *him* to forget it!

'I do. It's Jack Sprat!' said Susie, and Peter scowled at her. She was right. Jack Sprat was the last password they had chosen – a secret password – and here was Susie shouting it out in the road. She saw his angry face and laughed.

'I'm right, aren't I? Yours is a silly society. I know your password, and so do all the girls in my class. I told them. So the next time you have a meeting we'll all be along, shout out the password, and you'll have to let us in.'

'Who told you the password?' demanded Peter. 'I know Jack wouldn't.'

'Oh no. Jack's a most annoying brother. He never tells me anything,' said Susie. 'But when I went to borrow a hanky from his drawer, I found a piece of paper there, hidden under a pile of hankies. And on it was scribbled: "Remember the password – Jack Sprat".'

'You're always snooping about, Susie!' said Peter, angrily. 'I never knew such a girl. Why can't you leave us alone, and not keep trying to find out our passwords and what we're doing?'

'Well, why don't you let me belong?' demanded Susie. 'You let Janet belong, and Pam and Barbara.'

'Don't be silly. It's the Secret *Seven*. We can't have any more members, or we'd be eight,' said Peter. 'Anyway, we don't want you, Susie.'

'You're mean,' said Susie. 'Well, I'll tell Jack you're having another meeting soon. When shall I say it is?'

'Don't you go telling Jack anything!' said Peter, really exasperated with this annoying sister of Jack's. '*I* send out notices of meetings, not you. And you needn't bother to remember the password. I shall choose another one immediately, and let the members know.'

'Oh, well, Jack is sure to write it down to remember it again,' said Susie, skipping off. 'And I shall be sure to find it. Goodbye, and give my love to Jack Sprat.'

Peter glared at Susie's back. What an awful girl! He was glad that his own sister, Janet, wasn't like Susie. He walked home with a solemn face.

Certainly a meeting must be called soon. There hadn't been one for ages. It would never do to let the Secret Seven come to an end just because there weren't any meetings, or anything special happening.

But you can't solve mysteries and things unless there are some to solve, thought Peter. We'll have to think up something else to do, till one comes along. Sometimes it seems as if nothing happens for ages and ages. I'll have to change the password, too. Fancy Jack being such an idiot as to write down the password in case he forgot it. He might have known that Susie would find it.

He went home, thinking hard. Janet, his sister, was already there, and Scamper, the golden spaniel, came rushing out to greet him, barking with joy.

'Hallo, Scamper! Been a good dog today?' said Peter, fondling the long, silky ears. 'Eaten all your dinner? Been sniffing for rabbits? Barked at the dust-man? You have? Ah, you're a *very* good dog, then!'

'Woof!' said Scamper, and raced round the room like a mad dog.

Janet laughed. 'He knew you were coming long before you came in at the door,' she said. 'He sat with his head on one side, listening for about three minutes before you came in. He must have known when you turned the corner up the lane.'

'Janet,' said Peter, putting down his satchel of books. 'We've got to call a Secret Seven meeting as soon as possible.'

'Oh, good! But why? Has anything

happened?' said Janet, thrilled. She was disappointed when Peter shook his head.

'No – except that I met that awful sister of Jack's – Susie. And she's found out the password, and she was jeering at us because we haven't had a meeting for ages. So we simply must have one, and we must choose a new password, too! Get out your note-paper, and we'll arrange a meeting as soon as we can.'

[2]

Secret Seven meeting

The Secret Seven meeting was called for the very next day, immediately after school. Peter's mother was told, and she suggested that all the members should come to tea first, and have the meeting afterwards.

'I'll wash up every single thing after the meeting,' said Janet. 'Hurrah! Another Secret Seven meeting. How pleased everyone will be!'

The notes were sent out, and the Secret Seven were thrilled. Jack went scrabbling in his drawer to find the bit of paper on which he had written the password. He found it, but he was *most* surprised when he read it. This is what he read:

'Remember the password – Jack Sprat. No, Jack Horner. No, Jack the Giant-Killer. No – it's Jack and Jill!'

Jack stared at the bit of scribbled paper, frowning. Whatever had made him write all that? He must have been mad. And which was the password? He was sure it was Jack Sprat.

He looked closely at the paper. 'Bother Susie! She's written half of it! She's been snooping in my drawer and found the paper, and read the password! Just wait till I see her!'

But fortunately for Susie she was out to tea. Jack hunted for his badge, and at last found it. He had been afraid that Susie might have discovered that too. Really, she was the most annoying sister in the world!

The tea-party was fixed for half-past four, after school. Janet and Peter had carried everything down, and the shed looked very warm and cosy. They had a small oil-stove in one corner for warmth, six candles stuck here and there, and a box for a table. Janet had put a cloth on it.

Two enormous jugs of hot cocoa stood there, with seven mugs round it. Ranged on a shelf behind were seven plates of food.

'Honey sandwiches, sardine sandwiches – and I hope you won't go for those too much, Peter, you're a pig over sardines,' said Janet. 'Buns buttered and jammed, all in halves. New doughnuts. A chocolate cake baked today. A yummy jam-sponge sandwich, already cut into seven by Mummy. Doesn't it look lovely? Oh – and a plate of mixed biscuits.'

'Woof!' said Scamper at once, and his tail thumped hard on the ground.

'*Your* dish of goodies is on the floor, but you're not to begin your tea till we do,' said Janet. Scamper looked at his own plate and sniffed longingly.

He saw two sardine sandwiches, made of the tails and little bones; one bun cut in half, with just a scraping of butter, but no jam, because Scamper liked his without; and a very large dog-biscuit smeared with meat paste. What a tea for a hungry dog!

'Here they come,' said Janet, as they heard footsteps coming down the path to the shed. She peered out of the window. 'It's Pam and Barbara.'

Rap-rap!

'Password!' called out Peter.

'Jack Sprat,' came the answer, and Peter opened the door at once. No sooner was it shut than more footsteps were heard, and another knock.

'Password?'

'Er – I'm most awfully sorry, Peter, but it's such ages since we had a meeting that I've forgotten it,' said a voice, sounding rather upset. Janet glanced at Peter. Was he going to be cross, and perhaps refuse to let in poor Colin?

No. Peter didn't look at all cross. He opened the door, and Colin came in, looking most relieved.

'Hallo!' he said, staring in delight at the tea. 'I'm sorry about the password, but, honestly, it's ages since we used it.'

'It's all right,' said Peter. 'It was my fault for not calling a meeting before. Anyway, that awful sister of Jack's knows it, so we've got to choose a new one.'

Rap-rap-rap-RAP!

'Password!' called Peter.

'Jack Sprat!' said two voices, and in came George and Jack, complete with Secret Seven badges. The door shut. The candles gave a wavering light in the rather dark shed, and everything looked cosy, and rather mysterious. Just the kind of thing the Secret Seven liked!

'What's the meeting about?' said Jack,

sitting on an upturned flowerpot. 'Anything special?'

'No,' said Peter. 'Nothing's turned up, worse luck – but we can't let our Society fizzle out because we wait and wait for something to happen. We'll talk about that later. Pour out the cocoa, Janet, and remember that we all like heaps of sugar.'

'Woof! woof!' said Scamper, approvingly, and got a lump of sugar from Janet at once. She poured out the cocoa, and Peter handed round the sandwiches. Soon everyone was tucking in, and Scamper gulped down his sandwiches and his bun in no time, and then settled down happily to crunch his biscuit.

In ten minutes' time every plate was empty. Not even a biscuit was left. Jack sat back with a sigh. 'That was a scrumptious tea,' he said. 'Any more cocoa left?'

'Half a mug each,' said Janet. 'Pass yours up.'

'While we're having our last drink, we'll begin the meeting,' said Peter. 'It's not a very *important* meeting, but we've got quite a bit to discuss and to plan. If this Secret Seven hasn't any particular job to work on, it's got to find other things to do. Do you agree, members?'

'We do,' said everyone, pleased.

'Right,' said Peter. 'Well, I'll begin. Stop thumping your tail on the floor, Scamper, and you listen too!'

[3]

A new password – and a few ideas

Everyone sat quietly. Scamper stopped his tail-thumping and sat still too, his head on one side. He was very, very proud to be at all the meetings, even though he wasn't a proper member.

'First of all,' said Peter, 'we must choose a new password, partly because Susie knows it!'

Jack was startled. How did Peter know that Susie knew it? 'Yes, she does know it,' he said, and fished the piece of paper out of his pocket, on which he had written the old password, and on which Susie had scribbled her nonsense.

'Look there, she found this bit of paper,

with our password on it. I wrote it down so that I wouldn't forget it, and I hid it, and she found it and scribbled on it! But how did you *know* she knew it, Peter?'

'She told me,' said Peter. 'She seemed to think our Society was about to come to an end, or something, and she was so annoying that it made me decide to call a meeting at once. Jack, for goodness' sake don't leave our passwords about again!'

'All right. I won't,' said Jack, looking rather red in the face. 'But you don't know what it is to have a sister like Susie. I wouldn't be surprised if she isn't trying to peep in at the window this very minute.'

Everyone at once looked up at the little window, Scamper too. Peter shook his head.

'No, nobody's about. Scamper would bark if he heard the slightest sound. Well, what about a new password? Anyone got a good idea?'

'Snooper!' said Colin, thinking of Susie. 'That would be a good one.'

'Yes, we'd all remember that because of Susie,' said Janet.

'We'll have to remember the password is *Snooper*, not *Susie*,' said Pam, with a giggle. 'I'm sure I shall say "Susie" if anyone asks me the password next week!'

Jack often felt cross with his sister, but he didn't very much like the idea of the password being chosen because of Susie's snoopy behaviour. After all, she *was* his sister, and although she was very annoying at times, he was fond of her. He shook his head.

'No. I don't want that password, if you don't mind. I've got a better one. One that nobody would ever think of. What about "Beware!"? It sounds sort of *suitable* for us.'

'Yes, it does,' agreed Peter, and the others nodded their heads. They began to say the password to one another, in hollow, mysterious voices, and Scamper looked rather startled.

'Beware!' Janet said to Barbara, solemnly.

'Be-warrrrrrre!' hissed Colin to Jack.

'BEWARE!' said Peter to Scamper, who got up at once and sniffed in every corner of the shed, as if he had to discover what it was that everyone was warning him about. Beware! Well, he would beware all right, but what of?

'Look at Scamper. He's puzzled to bits,' said Pam, with a laugh. 'It's all right, Scamper. It's just our new password. Well, I don't think *any* of us will forget it. It's a very good one. Beware! It makes me feel quite creepy.'

'The next thing to discuss is what the Secret Seven are to do,' said Peter. 'I suppose nobody has heard of anything peculiar or mysterious or extraordinary that we could look into?'

Nobody said a word. They just looked at one another hopefully, and then shook their heads.

'Well, as there's nothing peculiar to make plans about, we'll have to decide something to *do*,' said Peter. 'I mean, it's been such a long time since we held a meeting, and societies just fizzle out if they're not kept going somehow. We must *do* something to keep up our interest or when something *does* come along, we'll miss it.'

'Yes, but what do you mean, *do* something?' asked Colin. 'We can't *make* things happen.'

'No. I know that,' said Peter. 'But we can put in a bit of practice. We can set ourselves one or two things to do.'

'What, for instance?' said George.

'Well, we could practise shadowing people,' said Peter. 'And we might perhaps have a shot at disguising ourselves, just to see if we could get away with it.'

'Disguising ourselves? But how could we?' said Pam. 'We're only children. We can't wear false beards, or ragged clothes, or pretend to walk with limps or anything. We'd be spotted at once.'

'Well, perhaps that's not such a good idea,' admitted Peter. 'We'll leave that for the minute. But we could practise spotting somebody, and then writing down a very clear description of him, so as to get practice at that kind of thing. It's always useful to be able to describe a thief in great detail, for instance.'

'But how do we know who's a thief?' said Jack.

'We don't,' said Peter, beginning to be impatient. 'We just go, say, to the railway station, and sit down on a seat. We watch the people standing there waiting for a train. We pick on somebody, it doesn't matter who. We look at them carefully, and memorise everything about them.

Then, when they've gone, we write down what we've remembered. It would be very, very good practice for observing people.'

'It sounds rather dull to me,' said George. 'I'd much sooner do some shadowing or something. Anyway, I'm not much good at describing anything. I'm always bottom in composition at school. I just can't think of a thing to say.'

'All right, you can do the shadowing,' said Peter. 'Perhaps the girls would be better at spotting people and describing them.'

'Woof!' said Scamper, suddenly. 'WOOF!'

'Somebody's about,' said Peter. 'Quick, open the door and let Scamper out. If it's Susie we'll give her the fright of her life!'

[4]

What fun to belong to a Secret Society!

It wasn't Susie. It was Peter's mother coming to say that it was getting late, and did they know what the time was? She was very surprised to meet Scamper flying out of the door in the greatest excitement, barking for all he was worth. He was quite disappointed that it was only Peter's mother!

'Oh, Mother, it *can't* be half-past six yet,' groaned Peter. 'We haven't nearly finished the meeting. Yes, I know we haven't done our homework, but we haven't much tonight. Can't we have another ten minutes?'

'Yes. Ten minutes, then,' said his mother, and went away. The door was shut again, and the Secret Seven began to talk hurriedly.

'George, you can do a spot of shadowing, and so can Colin,' said Peter. 'You girls can do the observation idea, go to the station or the bus stop, or anywhere. Jack, you and I will do a bit of spying. We'll find a good spying-place, sit there, and watch what goes on without being seen. It will be good practice for when we *really* have to do it!'

'How do we do the shadowing?' asked George. 'We'd be seen following anybody in broad daylight.'

'Well, do it when it's dark, then,' said Peter. 'But don't go shadowing anyone together, you and Colin, or you'll be spotted at once. That would be silly. Go separately, choose someone you see, and follow them to their home without being seen. If you can do that, you'll be very smart!'

'I'd rather tackle a *real* mystery or

problem than mess about practising,' said George, in a grumbling voice.

'I'm the head of this Society, and you have to obey orders,' said Peter in rather a haughty voice. 'I've got to keep the Secret Seven going, haven't I? Well, I'm doing my best.'

'Anyway, you never know when we *might* come across something when we're putting in a bit of practice in these things,' said Jack, cheerfully. 'Things pop up most unexpectedly.'

'We'll practise our observation stunt on Saturday morning,' said Janet. 'I'll go to the railway station. I always like that, it's nice and busy and noisy.'

'I'll go to the bus stop,' said Pam. 'You come with me, Barbara.'

'Right,' said Peter, pleased. 'Now we've all got secret jobs to do, and they'll keep us going till something turns up. Jack, I'll let you know when I've thought of a good place for us to hide and keep a watch on any goings-on nearby.'

Everyone got up, sorry that the meeting had come to an end. Pam and Barbara offered to help Janet wash up, and all the boys carried in the dirty plates and mugs for the girls.

'Now for homework,' said Peter, with a groan. 'I wish I'd listened better in class this morning. I haven't the faintest idea how to do those sums we've been set.'

Pam, Jack and George said good night, and thanked Peter's mother for the 'delicious' tea. The others washed up together, chattering at the tops of their voices. They didn't say a word of what had happened at the meeting, of course. Nobody was ever supposed to tell anything that had passed at one of the Secret Seven gatherings.

But all the members thought about it a lot. It was fun to belong to a Secret Society. It was something you could hug to yourself and think about before you went to sleep at night. Janet looked at her Secret Seven badge that evening when she took it off her dress.

'S.S.,' she said. 'It should really be *five* Ss. S.S.S.S.S. For Super, Smashing, Secret, Seven, Society! I must remember to tell Peter that. I'll go to the station on Saturday morning, and watch for someone to describe perfectly. I won't miss a thing, not even the colour of his tie! I'll show the others how good I am at noticing every single thing about somebody I see just for a minute.'

Peter was thinking about what he and Jack could do, too, as he lay in bed that night. A spyhole? Now, where would an *interesting* one be? In the middle of the bush beside the main road? Yes, that would be a good place. They could take notebooks and note down the cars that went by. They could put down anything they thought was interesting or suspicious. It would be fun!

Each member was planning carefully what he or she was to do. George was perhaps making the most careful plans of all. He was to go and shadow somebody. Well, he would do it really properly! He would first of all hide somewhere, and watch for somebody to come by. Then he would slip out and follow them, oh, so carefully and quietly! He would put on his rubber shoes.

And I'll creep behind in the shadows, just like a policeman following a thief or a spy! he thought. I'll be like a shadow myself. Nobody will know I'm there. I'll choose a man with a bag, to make it more real. I'll pretend he's got stolen maps in it, or jewels or something. Gosh, I'm going to enjoy this!

All the Seven fell asleep at last. What fun it was to belong to a Secret Society!

[5]

A little shadowing

'Peter, when is the next meeting, do you suppose?' asked Janet, on Saturday morning. 'I'm going to the station now, to do my practice for the Secret Seven, you know, watching somebody and describing them, and I'd like to know when I can give my work in to the Society. I'm going to do it really well.'

'Well, I'll call the meeting for one evening next week,' said Peter. 'That will be time enough. I'm going off now to find a good spyhole with Jack. Have I got my notebook and pencil? Yes, I have. Well, good luck at the station, Janet, and don't choose just one person. That would be too easy. Choose three at least.'

'I thought I'd choose somebody we all know, too, if I can,' said Janet. 'Then you'll see if you can recognise them when I read out my notes.'

'Good idea,' said Peter. 'Well, I'm off to call for Jack.'

He set off, and Janet went in the opposite direction, to the station. She passed Barbara and Pam on the way. They were sitting on the bus-stop seat, looking rather giggly, with notebooks in their hands.

'Have you begun yet?' asked Janet, in a low voice.

'No. No bus has stopped here yet,' said Pam. 'We're each going to choose one passenger getting out, and wait till the bus has gone off again. Then we're going to put down exactly what we remember about the two passengers.'

Colin and George were not thinking about their Secret Seven jobs just then. Both had decided to do them at night. Shadowing would be so much easier then. They were not going together, of course. Peter had forbidden that.

But when the evening came, only George set out. Colin had sneezed three times, and his mother had heard him. As she knew he caught colds very easily, she wouldn't let him go out after tea!

'But, Mother, I *must*,' said Colin, desperately. 'It's Secret Seven work. I've *got* to do it.'

'Can't it be done another night?' said his mother. 'Surely it isn't absolutely necessary to do it tonight.'

Colin hesitated. 'Well, yes, I suppose it *could* be done another night,' he said truthfully. 'All right, Mother, I won't go tonight. But you *will* let me go another night, won't you?'

So only George went out shadowing that night. He had put on rubber shoes so that he made no sound when walking or running. He had put on a dark overcoat, so that he wouldn't be seen in the shadows. He had even blacked his face. He looked most peculiar!

He stared at himself in the mirror and grinned, so that his teeth suddenly showed startlingly white in his black face. 'I'd better slip out of the garden door,' he decided. 'If Mother catches sight of me she'll have a fit! I do look strange!'

He decided to take a rubber truncheon that he had had for Christmas, to make it seem more real. Now I can really pretend I'm a policeman! he thought, swinging the rubber truncheon from his wrist. It looked exactly like a real one, but was only made of thin brown rubber!

He crept downstairs and out of the garden door. His rubber shoes made no sound. He went down the path to the back gate and came out quietly into the dark street. The street lamps were lit. He would have to keep out of their radiance.

He went along cautiously, swinging the rubber truncheon. Now then, you thieves! Now then, you spies! Look out, here comes P.C. Rubber-Soles, hard on your trail!

Who was he to shadow? Nobody seemed to come along at all. Wait a minute, was this the bus coming? Yes, it was. Good! It would set some passengers down, and he could trail one of them to his home, wherever it was.

The bus stopped up the street, and George saw some black shadows moving as people stepped down from it. Somebody was walking towards him now, having got off the bus. He would shadow him! George pressed himself back into the hedge, and waited, scarcely daring to breathe.

The man came along. He was a tall, stooping fellow, wearing a hat, and carrying a bag. Good! Suppose there were stolen jewels in that bag! George would trail him right to his home, and he would then know where this supposed robber lived!

It seemed very real somehow, not pretence. The night was dark, the man came along without guessing that a boy was pressing himself into the shadows of a bush, and George suddenly found his heart beginning to thump. The man passed.

Now to follow him without being seen. If he spotted George, then George had failed. But George was certain he could shadow the man right back to his house without once being seen.

He came out from the bush and began to follow the man, keeping well into the darkness of the trees that lined the road. Down the road to the corner. Round the corner. Be careful now, *creep* round the corner, in case the man knows he is being followed!

George crept round cautiously, his rubber truncheon in his hand, pretending to himself that there might be great danger from a fierce thief!

He heaved a sigh of relief. There was the man, half-way down the road. George trotted on after him. Look behind you, George, as well as in front. Quick, George, look behind you!

[6]

A shock for poor George

But George didn't look behind him. He only looked in front, and followed the man steadily. Once, when he stopped to tie his shoelace, George darted into a near-by gate, afraid that the man might turn and see him.

He crept out after half a minute, and saw the man walking on again, swinging his bag. After him went George, deciding to get a little nearer, so that he could see exactly where the man lived when he went into his house.

So he crept quite near, feeling very bold and successful. And then suddenly something happened.

George heard sudden footsteps behind

him, and then a heavy hand fell on his shoulder and a sharp voice spoke loudly.

'And what do you think *you* are doing, creeping along in the dark after that gentleman in front? What's this you've got on your wrist? A truncheon! Don't tell me you meant to use it, you wicked little scoundrel!'

George was so astounded that he couldn't say a word. He stared up at the man, who dragged him to a nearby lamp-post.

'What have you done to your face?' said the man.

He was a young fellow, strong and very determined-looking, and he gave George a sudden shake.

'Have you lost your tongue?' He dabbed at George's face, and whistled. 'You've blacked it. What for? Are you one of the wretched little hooligans who think they can hit innocent people, rob them and run away?' demanded the young man, and shook George roughly again.

George found his tongue. 'Let me go!' he said, indignantly. 'Of course I'm not a hooligan! I'm only shadowing somebody for, well, just for practice!'

'I don't believe a word of it,' said the man. 'I've followed you right from the bus, you little wretch! I watched you hiding here and there, creeping round the corners, following that old fellow with the bag. Come along with me. I'll take you to the police station. You can tell your tale there!'

George was really frightened now. He tried to wriggle away, but the man held him too tightly.

'Please don't take me to the police station,' begged George. 'My mother would be so upset. Take me home. I'll tell you my name and address, and come with you. You'll see I'm a good boy, not a hooligan. I wouldn't DREAM of following anyone to rob them.'

'All right. I'll take you to your home,'

said the young man, grimly. 'And I'll have a word with your father, young man. What you want is a good talking to!'

And poor George had to trot beside him all the way home, held so tightly by his collar that he could hardly breathe.

He didn't have at all a pleasant time at home. The young man made his harmless adventure seem very, very serious. His mother was shocked. His father was angry.

'Well, I didn't mean any harm,' said poor George, rather sulky now. 'It was only the orders I had from Peter, who is the head of the Secret Seven, our society. We were just practising several things, in case some mystery or other turned up. That's all. I had to shadow someone, and I did. But there wasn't any *harm* in it!'

'I see,' said his father. 'Well, that's the end of the Secret Society for you, George. If I'm going to have you hauled home by a member of the public, accusing you of following some harmless old fellow, and carrying a truncheon, and with your face blacked, well, all I can say is that the Secret Society is leading you into bad ways.'

'I agree,' said his mother. 'He mustn't belong any more.'

George looked at his parents in the utmost dismay. 'But Dad! Mother! You don't understand. I couldn't *possibly* not belong to the Secret Seven. They wouldn't let me go. I *must* belong!'

'That's enough, George,' said his father, curtly. 'You know I won't be argued with. Go and wash that black off your face, and tell this Secret Society of yours tomorrow that you no longer belong. Do you hear me?'

'Yes, Dad,' said George, shocked and miserable. He said good night in a low voice, gave the young man a fearful scowl, and went out of the room. He debated whether to slam the door or not, but decided not to. His father did not look kindly on any show of temper.

Poor George! He washed his black face, undressed, and got into bed. What a dreadful thing not to belong to the Secret Seven any more! What would they do without him? They would only be Six. Would they call themselves the Secret Six? That would still be S.S.

Or, dreadful thought, would they get someone else instead of him? George felt as if he really could *not* bear that. He buried his face in his pillow and gritted his teeth. It was too bad! He had only done what Peter had told him, and he had done it very well too, and that horrid young man had thought he was up to mischief and had hauled him home.

Tomorrow he must go and tell Peter and Janet. They would have to call a meeting on Monday night and decide what to do without him. He would be there for the last time.

He would never, never attend one of those exciting secret meetings after that.

'I shall howl if I go on thinking like this,' said George fiercely, and hit his pillow hard, pretending it was the young man who had caught him. 'Take that! And that!'

He felt better then, but it was a long time before he fell asleep. Poor George!

[7]

George resigns – and a new member is elected

On Monday evening, immediately after school, a meeting of the Secret Seven was called. All the Seven knew why. It was about George.

George had gone to see Peter on Sunday morning, and had told him what had happened. Peter was shocked.

'We must call a meeting as soon as possible,' he said, 'to see what we can do about it. Poor George! This is awful!'

So a very solemn, serious meeting was held down in the little shed that had the S.S. sign on its door. George gave the password in rather a trembling voice as he went in, and wore his badge for the last time.

'Beware!' he said, and as he spoke the door was opened. Everyone was there, Scamper as well.

'Hallo, George,' said Janet, feeling very miserable to see George's woebegone face. 'Bad luck!'

'I expect Peter's told you what happened,' said George, sitting down on a box. 'It was just, well, what Janet said just now, bad luck!'

George took off his badge and handed it to Peter, who pinned it carefully to his jersey, beside his own badge.

'I now resign from the Secret Seven,' said George, in rather a shaky voice. 'Thank you for letting me belong. I'm very, very sorry to go, but my father says I must.'

'It's horrid of him!' said Pam fiercely, very sorry for George.

But George was not going to have anything said against his father, much as he resented being forced to leave the Secret Seven.

'He's not horrid,' he said, loyally. 'It was that young man's fault. He caused all the trouble, making such a fuss about me. He *knew* I wasn't doing any harm. He's the mean, horrid one, not my father.'

'Who was he? Do you know?' asked Jack.

'No idea,' said George. 'I'd never seen him before. When Dad asked him for his address, he said that he lived at that little hotel called "Starling's". He didn't give his name.'

'I've a good mind to go and find out who he is and tell him what I think of him!' said Jack, scowling.

'Yes. That's a good idea,' said Peter. 'Colin, Jack and I will all go. It's the least we can do for old George. We'll tell that young man what we think of him!'

'He'll just haul you home too, and get *you* into trouble!' said George, feeling rather comforted by all the interest on his behalf. 'I must say I couldn't understand why he was so interfering. Even when I told him who I was and where I lived, he was just as mean.'

'Starling's Hotel,' said Peter, and wrote it down firmly in his notebook. 'We'll go and ask for him and tell him he's done a really mean thing.'

'I'll come, too,' said Pam, bravely; but Peter said no, the three of them could manage by themselves.

'What are you going to do about the Secret Seven now?' asked George after a pause. 'I mean, you're only six, now I'm out of it. Will you be the Secret Six?'

'No,' said Peter. 'We began as the Secret Seven, and we'll have to go on as the Secret Seven. You can't suddenly change a society as important as ours.'

'I see,' said George. 'Well, you'll have to get a seventh, then. I shall hate that. Who will you have? Lennie, or Richard?'

'No,' said Peter, firmly, and everyone looked at him to see who was in his mind.

'Hadn't we better all put up somebody's name, and then we'll vote?' asked Colin. 'That's if we've got to have someone else. I shan't much like anyone in George's place.'

'You will ALL like the one that I'm thinking of, I promise you,' said Peter, and his eyes twinkled at them. 'Nobody will say no, I promise you!'

'Who is it?' said poor George, wondering who this wonderful person was that everyone would welcome.

'Yes, who is it?' said Janet, puzzled.

'He's with us tonight,' said Peter. 'But he will only be a temporary member, not a member for good, just a temporary member till we get George back again. Because I'm determined to go and find that young man and make him go and ask George's parents to let him belong to the Secret Seven again. I bet he didn't know how important it is to George to belong.'

'But who's the temporary member?' said George, puzzled. He looked all round. 'There's nobody here but us.'

'It's Scamper!' said Peter, and Scamper leapt up at his name, and wagged his tail vigorously. 'Scamper, will you please be a proper member of the Secret Seven till we get George back?'

'Woof, *woof*, WOOF!' said Scamper, joyously, as if he understood completely. Everyone began to laugh, even George.

'Oh, Peter!' he said, 'Scamper's the only person I don't mind taking my place! He's always *really* belonged to the Secret Seven, hasn't he? Oh, I do hope I come back. Still, I don't feel so bad now that Scamper's the seventh member. I just felt I couldn't bear to know that Lennie or Richard belonged instead of me.'

Everybody felt more cheerful. Scamper

ran round and licked all the knees and hands he could see.

'Just as if he's saying "Thank you, thank you for this great honour,"' said Jack. 'Good old Scamper! Peter, pin the badge to his collar. Scamper, please remember the password. Let me say it in your ear, BEWARE!'

The meeting broke up. George said goodbye rather solemnly. Scamper took the members proudly to the gate, and then turned back. Wait till he showed the other dogs his magnificent badge!

[8]

A few reports

Another Secret Seven meeting was held the next night, to hear the result of the various 'observations' and 'watchings'. All the seven were there, but the seventh this time was Scamper, not George. It seemed strange without him.

It was quite a business-like meeting. Janet spoke first. She took out her notebook and read from it.

'I was at the railway station,' she said, 'and I picked out three people to observe as they passed. They came off the ten–thirteen train from Pilberry.'

'First, an old woman with a round face, a big nose with a wart at one side, and grey curly hair. She wore a green coat with a belt, a hat with lots of red cherries round it and—'

'Mrs Lawson!' yelled everyone at once, and Janet looked pleased.

'Yes,' she said. 'Quite right. I chose her just to see if I could describe her well enough for you to recognise. Here's the second person, not very exciting. A young woman in a nurse's uniform, golden hair, doll-like face, small feet and a quick walk.'

'Well, it's quite a good *short* description,' said Peter. 'I feel as if I might know her if I saw her. I think you're good at this, Janet.'

Janet went red with pleasure. She loved Peter to praise her. 'Here's my last,' she said. 'I chose him because he really was a bit peculiar. Listen.

'A very stoopy man, who walked a bit lame, had an old soft hat pulled well down over his face, a long overcoat with the shouiders very square, small feet for his size, a funny hand—'

'What do you mean, a funny hand?' asked Peter.

'Well, I don't quite know what was the matter with it,' said Janet. 'It looked as if two fingers were missing, and it was sort of deformed and crooked. That's all.'

'Colour of his hair, his tie or scarf, and how did he walk – quick, slow or medium?' asked Peter.

'His hat was too low, I couldn't see his hair, and he had no tie or scarf,' said Janet. 'And he limped a bit. There! Do you think you would recognise *him* if you saw him?'

'Oh yes!' said everyone. 'Well done, Janet.'

'Now you, Barbara and Pam,' said Peter. But their notes proved to be rather silly.

'They sound as if you'd had one of your stupid giggling fits,' said Peter, reprovingly. 'Don't read any more. They wouldn't be a *bit* of use if we were *really* trying to find out something. Very poor, both of you. Now you, Colin. Did you do any shadowing?'

'No,' said Colin. 'I began a cold on Saturday night, so my mother wouldn't let me. I'm doing it tonight, after this meeting. I'm sorry, but it wasn't my fault.'

'Right,' said Peter. 'Well, that only leaves me and Jack. We found a good spyhole in a thick clump of leafy twigs springing out round the trunk of a great elm tree. They hid us beautifully. We sat there, peeping through the leaves, and at first we saw nothing.'

'Not many people walk along that road,' explained Jack. 'It's Fairmile Road, and you know how long it is. Most people take a bus. We didn't see anyone for ages.'

'In fact, we haven't much to report,' said Peter. 'The only possible thing of interest we saw was a car that came by, and stopped just near us.'

'But why was that interesting?' asked Pam.

'Well, it *wasn't* very interesting, actually,' said Peter. 'All that happened was that a man got out with a dog, a magnificent grey poodle, fluffy in patches and bare in patches, you know how poodles look! The dog was terribly frightened, I thought. But you could see it was only car-sick and it soon recovered, and began to sniff round quite naturally.'

'It didn't like going back into the car, though,' said Jack. 'It whined like anything and pulled away from the man as hard as it could. He was pretty rough with it, I thought.'

'I suppose the poor thing knew it would be car-sick again,' said Janet. 'Do you remember our next-door neighbour's dog, Peter? Every time it went out in the car, it cried and cried because it felt so ill.'

'Well your report doesn't seem *very* interesting,' said Barbara, rather glad to repay Peter for his candid remarks about her report and Pam's. 'Did you take the car's number? I bet you didn't.'

'There wasn't much point in taking it,' said Peter. 'But as it happens, we did. Here it is – PSD 188.'

'PSD – pretty sick dog!' said Colin. 'That's easy enough to remember!'

There was a laugh, and then a pause. Peter shut his notebook.

'Well that's all,' he said. 'I don't really feel we've done very much that is useful. Janet's reports are the best. They show how good she would be if she had to describe someone seen for only half a minute. The police are always asking for descriptions of persons seen by the public, and hardly anyone ever seems to be able to remember much about any stranger they saw.'

'But Janet would be able to tell them everything,' said Pam, rather jealously.

'The only big thing that has come out of this practice idea is George having to leave the Secret Seven,' said Colin, gloomily. 'Well, is it worthwhile my doing my bit of shadowing tonight, Peter? I mean, we don't seem to have done anything much, and I don't want to get caught like George.'

'George should have looked behind him as well as in front,' said Peter. 'You won't make that mistake. I think you should do your bit, Colin. I've a good mind to make Pam and Barbara do their bits again too!'

But the girls looked so crossly at him that he decided to say no more!

Colin got up. 'Well, I'm going on my job,' he said. 'What are you all going to do?'

'Let's go indoors and play a game,' suggested Janet. 'There are five of us left – sorry, Scamper, six – I forgot you! We've got an hour before it's supper-time. Come along in, Pam, Barbara and Jack.'

So they all five went in, and were soon playing a peaceful game of cards. But it wasn't peaceful for long! Who was that rapping at the window?

Tap-tap-tap! Tap-tap-tap!

'Quick! Open the window. I've something to tell you all!'

[9]

Colin's strange tale

'Open the window!' said Janet, putting down her cards. 'It's Colin! What's happened?'

Peter opened the window, and Colin climbed in. He was panting. 'Thanks,' he said. 'I didn't like to come to the front door or the back, in case your mother saw me and asked me what was up. So I tapped at the window. I saw you inside, playing cards.'

'What's happened?' said Peter. 'You're dirty, and your hand's bleeding.'

'Oh, that's nothing,' said Colin. 'Listen! You know I left you to go and find somebody to shadow, don't you?'

'Yes,' said everyone.

'Well, I didn't see anyone at first,' said Colin, 'and it began to rain and I was pretty fed up. So I chose to shadow the very first person I saw.'

'Who was that?' said Jack.

'A young man with a dog,' said Colin. 'I thought he must be taking it out for an evening walk. It didn't seem to like the walk very much. It kept whining and pulling away from the man, and I thought it might smell me, following quietly along some way behind, but it didn't seem to. I couldn't see what the dog was like at first, because it's a dark evening and raining. Then, when the man and the dog walked beneath a street lamp, I saw it.'

'What was it?' asked Janet.

'It was a bull-terrier,' said Colin. 'A beauty. A real beauty. My mother's friend breeds them, so I know a good one when I see it. Well, I shadowed the man and the dog, and it was really pretty easy, because the man was so much taken up with the dog, having to drag it along, that he hadn't time to notice I was following him!'

'Go on. What happened to get you so excited?' said Peter, impatiently.

'I'm coming to that,' said Colin. 'I followed them down Hartley Street and across Plain Square, and into a little dark alley that led between some big buildings. I went down the alley cautiously, because I couldn't see my way very well, and daren't put on my torch.'

'Was the man there?' asked Jack.

'Let me tell my story in my own way,' said Colin. 'I'm just coming to the strange part. I went right down the alley, and just as I was nearly at the end, I heard the man coming back. I knew it was him because he has the same kind of quick dry cough my grandpa has, and he was coughing as he came.'

'What did you do?' said Janet, as he stopped for breath.

'I squashed myself into a doorway,' said Colin, 'and the man walked right by without seeing me. But he hadn't got the dog with him. So I wondered where he had put it, and why he had gone down there and come straight back again. So I went to the end of the alley myself and switched on my torch.'

'And was the dog there?' asked Pam.

'No,' said Colin. 'The alley led into a little yard, surrounded entirely by high walls. It was a messy place, full of rubbish. I flashed my torch all round, expecting to see the dog somewhere, tied up, perhaps, or even in a kennel, but there wasn't a sign of it!'

'Where was it, then?' asked Janet, after a pause.

'That's what I don't know,' said Colin. 'I looked absolutely everywhere for that dog. I listened for him, I called softly, but no, not a growl, not a whine, not a movement. And when I tell you that there was no way out of that yard except by that narrow alley, you'll guess how puzzled I was. I mean, a dog can't just *disappear* can it?'

'Woof!' said Scamper, exactly as if he was saying 'No!'

'I hunted all over that horrible yard,' said Colin. 'That's why I'm so dirty. And I cut my hand on some wire. But I tell you, there was no sign of that lovely bull-terrier, and no door or gate or anything for him to get out of. Then where was he? What had that man done with him, and why? It just beats me. I just *had* to come back and tell you.'

'There's something funny about this,' said Peter. 'I vote we go to that yard to-morrow and explore it. If there is some hiding-place there for a dog, we'll find it!'

'What a pity George isn't in this too,' said Janet. 'Peter, do go to that hotel and tell that young man he's got to go and tell George's parents they're to let him join the Secret Seven again. He'll be so upset when he knows we may be mixed up in something odd again and he won't be there to share in it.'

'All right, we'll go tomorrow after school,' said Peter. 'And then we'll go and explore that yard!'

'Yes, dogs don't just disappear,' said Jack. 'I expect there's a kennel there, or something, that you didn't notice in the dark, Colin.'

'Pooh!' said Colin. 'I'll give you fifty pence out of my money-box if you find a kennel there. You just see!'

[10]

The young man at Starling's

So, after school the next afternoon, Colin, Jack and Peter set off to go to Starling's Hotel, to see if they could find the young man who had hauled George home the other night and caused him to leave the Secret Seven.

They discussed what to say to him. 'We'll tell him the marvellous things that the Secret Seven have done,' said Peter. 'He'll soon see that a Society that can do the things we've done would only have decent boys and girls as members. I might tell him to go and ask the police about us. They would stick up for us like anything, because we've helped them so much.'

At last they came to Starling's. It was

rather a poor little hotel. There was a woman in the hall, and Peter asked her politely if there was a young man staying there. If so, could they please speak to him?

'What's his name?' asked the woman.

'We don't know,' said Peter.

'Well, what's he like?' said the woman, sounding impatient.

'We, we don't know that either,' said Peter, feeling foolish, and wishing that he had asked George for a description of the man. 'All we know is that he's young.'

'Oh well, I suppose it's Mr Taylor you want,' said the woman, ungraciously. 'He's the only young man staying here. Go into that room and I'll ask him to come and speak to you.'

They went into a tiny room and stood about awkwardly. Soon a young man came in and eyed the three boys curiously. 'What do you want?' he said.

Peter explained. 'It's about George, our

friend,' he said. 'The boy you caught the other night. You thought he was up to no good, but actually he was only putting in a bit of shadowing practice. He belonged to our Secret Society, you see, and we do all kinds of things. George's parents have told him he's not to belong, so—'

'Well, it's nothing to do with me,' said the young man. 'I can't do anything. He shouldn't play the fool.'

'He wasn't,' said Peter, warming up. 'I tell you, we're a very well-known society here, the police know us well; we've helped them many a time.'

'What rubbish!' said the young man.

'You ring up the Inspector and ask about us, then!' said Jack, indignantly.

The young man seemed rather astonished at this. He stared at Jack as if wondering whether to find out about them from the police or not.

'Well, whether you are friends with the

police or not, I'm not having any more to do with your friend George, or whatever his name is,' said the young man. 'So that's that. He's got no right to shadow people, whether in play or not. Now clear out, all of you.'

Colin hadn't said a word. He had been eyeing the young man closely, and Peter wondered why. Was he trying to do as the girls had done, and 'observe' someone closely so that he could describe him later?

As they went out, gloomy and resentful, a dog barked somewhere.

Colin turned to the young man. 'Is that your dog barking?' he asked.

'What dog? No! I haven't got a dog. And it wouldn't be any good if I had,' said the young man. 'They're not allowed in this hotel.'

Colin said no more, and the three boys walked out of the little hotel. They said nothing till they were well beyond the gate.

'He's hateful!' burst out Peter. 'Horrible cold eyes and thin mouth! As soon as I saw him I knew he was the kind of person that likes to get people into trouble. We once had a horrid teacher at school who had a mouth just like that!'

'Colin, why didn't you help us?' said Jack, as they walked down the road. 'You never said a word, till you asked about the dog that barked. Did you *have* to be unfriendly like that? You might have backed us up.'

'Wait a minute, I'll soon tell you why,' said Colin, and then the others saw that he was bursting to say something. 'Let's get right out of sight and hearing of Starling's first.'

They walked on for a while, and then Colin spoke in a low voice.

'That fellow, that young man, *he was the same one I saw last night* with the dog that disappeared!'

Jack and Peter stopped in surprise. 'What! Are you sure? But you asked him if it was his dog that was barking, and he said no he hadn't a dog!' Peter blurted all this out in far too loud a voice. Colin was afraid the passers-by might hear and he nudged Peter's arm.

'Be quiet. This may be important. Don't let's give anything away.'

'It's very interesting,' said Peter. 'Let's go to that yard at once and explore. We know the young man is safely at Starling's. He won't disturb us.'

'Come on, then,' said Colin. 'Oh, *bother*! Here's Susie.'

And Susie it was, coming at them like a hurricane, all out of breath. 'Peter! I've heard that George isn't in the Secret Seven any more. Please, PLEASE let me in! Jack, tell Peter to let me be in.'

'Certainly *NOT*,' said all three boys at once. 'We've got a seventh member already, thank you,' said Peter, remembering Scamper thankfully.

'Oh, bother! I did hope I'd be in time,' said Susie, and sailed off at top speed.

'What *cheek*!' said Jack. 'Honestly, she's the limit. Come on, let's go to this yard before Susie thinks of following us. Of all the *cheek*!'

The three boys set off in the direction of the yard that Colin had told them about.

'Hartley Street first,' said Colin, 'then across Plain Square. We come to the poorer parts of the town then.'

It took them a quarter of an hour to get to Plain Square, for Starling's Hotel was away at the other end of the town. They crossed the square, and then Colin looked for the alley-way leading between high buildings.

'There seem to be two or three,' said Peter. 'Which one was it, Colin?'

Colin hesitated. 'It all looks so different in the daylight,' he said. 'I think it's that one.

But I'll soon know when we get to the yard. I'll never forget that yard, rubbishy, dirty place it was!'

They chose an alley-way, and went down it. It came out into a small enclosure that had evidently been made into a playground for children. Some little girls were there, riding tricycles and pushing prams. They stared at the three boys.

'Not this one,' said Colin, and they went back down the alley. They chose the next one and went down that. 'I think this is the one,' said Colin. 'Here's the doorway I hid in to let the young man pass!'

They came to the end of the alley and Colin gave an exclamation. 'Yes! This is the yard. I recognise that pile of old boxes, and that broken-down rusty pram. This is where the man took the dog, disposed of it somewhere, and came back without it.'

The boys gazed round. High walls enclosed the little yard. A few dusty windows overlooked it, and Peter suddenly wondered if anyone would open a window and yell to them to clear out.

'Listen,' he said, in a low voice. 'We'd better be looking for our ball, or something, in case somebody gets suspicious of us and turns us away before we've discovered anything. Anyone got a ball?'

Colin had, a very small ping-pong ball, but it would do! He carefully dropped it in among some rubbish, and then the boys pretended to hunt for it. But really they were hunting for any place where a dog might have been put.

They turned that yard upside down, growing bolder as nobody disturbed them. It was a very quiet, lonely little yard, completely enclosed, with no outlet but the alley-way, and had obviously been used for a dumping place for old boxes, crates, broken crockery, sacks, sheets of cardboard and other things.

'Everything here but the dog!' said Peter at last. 'I think we've looked into every crate and box, and into every corner where a dog could be, though no dog would keep quiet if it heard us three rummaging about. There *must* be some outlet here besides that alley-way, an outlet big enough for a dog, any-way.'

They had moved every crate and box away from the walls, hoping to find some small door, but apparently the high walls contained no opening of any kind. It was a mystery!

Jack sat down on a big box in the middle of the yard to rest. Colin fell on him in one of his sudden silly fits, and began to wrestle with him, trying to get him off the box. Both boys fell over, and the box turned over too.

'Shut up,' said Peter, crossly. 'That box made quite a crash, turning over like that.'

Colin and Jack got up, brushing the dust off themselves, and grinning. Then Peter gave a cry. He clutched Jack's arm, and pointed down at his feet.

'Look – see that? What about *that* for pushing a dog through?'

All three were now staring down at Jack's feet. He was standing on an iron lid, a perfectly round one that fitted over what must have been a coal-hole.

'It was under that box, well hidden,' said Peter, excited. 'About the only box we didn't move, I should think. But who would have thought a coal-hole was under it? We didn't really *think* of a coal-hole, anyhow! Get off it, Jack, and let's have a look at it.'

Jack stepped off the round lid, and they all knelt down to look closely at it. 'It's been moved recently,' said Peter. 'It's not as caked with dirt round the edges as it should be. I bet that bull-terrier was shoved through here, Colin; I bet he was!'

'But why push a lovely dog down through a coal-hole?' said Colin, puzzled.

'What an extraordinary thing to do! And it seems a bit odd to me to have a coal-hole in this little yard. No coal-cart can come up that alley-way.'

'But a coal-man with a sack of coal can, stupid!' said Peter. 'Can we get this lid up? I'd like to peep down, and see if there's anything to be seen!'

It was an awkward thing to get up, besides being extremely heavy. Peter got very cross with it. But at last it was lifted, and shoved to one side. Then the boys all bent over eagerly, to look down. Their heads cracked together.

'I get first look,' said Peter, firmly. 'I'm the chief.' So the others let him look first.

He sat back, disappointed. 'Well, it's as dark and black as a, well as a coal-hole!' he said. 'Can't see a single thing. Anyone got a torch?'

'I've still got mine on me,' said Colin, and got it out of his pocket. They shone it down the dark hole. But even the light of the torch showed them nothing. Certainly there was no sign of a dog!

There was no sign of coal or coke either. It looked just a dark, horrible, deep hole.

'Er – anyone like to jump down?' said Peter.

[11]

The coal-hole

Nobody wanted to jump down in the least. For one thing, the hole wasn't very big – for another, the dark ground was a long way below – and for a third thing, who knew what might lie in wait for any daring boy dropping down through that hole!

'Well, I must say I think it would be rather silly to get down there, knowing as little as we do about this affair,' said Peter, at last. 'Do you suppose this is where the dog was pushed down, Colin?'

'I don't know,' said Colin, puzzled. 'The dog's not there now, anyway, dead or alive. The hole is empty. I suppose it's really an underground cellar, and may be quite big. Anyway, what's the point of pushing a lovely dog down a coal-hole? It doesn't make sense to me.'

'We'd better put the lid back and go home,' said Peter. 'It's getting dark. I'm not sure I like this nasty lonely little yard now it's getting towards night-time!'

He took hold of the lid, but Colin stopped him. 'Wait a minute,' he said. 'I've got an idea.'

He put his head right down into the hole. Then he whistled. Colin had a very shrill, piercing whistle that usually went right through people's heads making them angry. His shrill whistle sounded now, though it could not be very well heard up in the yard, because Colin's head was in the hole. It could be heard down in the cellar, though, for the piercing noise echoed round and round!

'What are you doing that for?' began Peter, angrily, but Jack guessed, and nudged him to be quiet. Colin was now listening, his head still down the hole. He heard something – what was it? Yes, there it came again. Then it stopped.

He took his head out, his eyes shining. 'The dog's down there somewhere all right,' he said. 'It heard my whistle, and I heard it barking, far away, somewhere, goodness knows where.'

'Gosh! Did you really?' said Peter, amazed. 'That was a really good idea of yours, Colin. Well, we now know for certain that the dog's down there, so that man must have pushed him into the hole. This is a mystery all right.'

'Yes. One that has sprung up all of a sudden, as mysteries usually do,' said Colin. 'What do we do next? We could get down the hole if we brought a rope-ladder, but we'll break our legs if we just try to *drop* down.'

There was a pause. The boys sat back on their bent knees and thought hard.

'The cellar must belong to one of these buildings,' said Jack, at last. 'But which one? It might belong to any of these around us. The coal-hole is exactly in the centre of the yard.'

'I can't see that it matters which one,' said Peter.

'Well, it might,' said Jack. 'We could find out if any firm in these buildings is interested in dogs.'

'Well, I suppose that's an idea,' said Peter, doubtfully. 'Anyway, let's put this lid back now, and place the box over it. We don't want anyone to suspect we've come across part of their secret.'

They put back the lid as quietly as they could, and dragged the box across it. Now it was as well-hidden as when they had first come into the yard.

'It's almost dark now,' said Peter. 'We'd better get back home. My mother will be wondering where I am – and oh, bother –

I've not done my homework yet. It's awfully difficult to swot at French verbs when you're thinking out a mystery all the time.'

'Look!' said Jack, as they turned to leave the yard. 'Look! Only one of these buildings has a lit window. Do you suppose the coal-cellar belongs to that one? Do you think there's anyone looking after that bull-terrier? He must be scared stiff if he's all by himself.'

The boys stared up at the lit window.

'It's the building on the left,' said Peter. 'It will be just round the corner of the block. Let's go that way and see what firm uses it. It might be a help, though, of course, the lit window may have nothing whatever to do with the mystery!'

They left the yard cautiously, went down the dark alley-way, and out into the street. They walked round the block, and came to the building that they thought must have shown the lit window. Colin switched his torch on to the dirty brass plate in the main doorway.

'Alliance of Callinated Sack Manufacturers!' he read. 'What on earth does that mean? Anyway, by the look of the building, the sack manufacturers must have gone west long ago. What a desolate, dirty place! It hasn't had a touch of paint for years!'

'It may be one of the buildings that the Council plan to pull down,' said Jack. 'I know some of them round about here are being pulled down, they're so old. Come on, let's go.'

'Look!' said Peter suddenly, and pulled the others to one side. 'The door's opening!'

Sure enough it was. The boys stood quietly in the shadows, waiting. Someone came out and shut the door softly. He went down the few steps into the street. He kept close to the wall as he walked along, a tall, stooping man.

With one accord the boys followed, their

rubber shoes making no sound. They knew that a lamp-post was round the corner. Perhaps they could see this man more clearly in the lamplight. Who was he?

'We'll shadow him!' whispered Peter. 'Come on.'

[12]

Two interesting encounters

The man came into the light of the street lamp, but only for a second. Peter tried to take in everything at one glance. He suddenly thought that Janet would have been very good at that!

The man went past the lamp, and into the darkness again.

Couldn't see very much, really, thought Peter. He had his hat pulled so well down over his face. He seems to limp a bit. Bother, I'd never recognise him again!

The man got along pretty quickly. He was making for the bus stop. It was easy for the boys to shadow him, because now other people were walking in the street too.

'He's making for the bus stop,' said Colin.

'We'll see which bus he catches. Shall we get on it, and look at him more carefully?'

'Yes,' said Peter, forgetting the lateness of the evening, forgetting his homework, in fact forgetting everything except for the excitement of the moment. They were on the track of a new mystery. How could anyone stop in the middle of it and go home!

The man made for the second of the two buses that were standing at the stop.

'It's the bus for Pilberry,' said Peter. 'Come on, we'll get on too.'

The man put out his hand to the bus-rail and swung himself up. Other people followed. The boys began to get on too, but the conductor put out his arm.

'Sorry,' he said. 'Full up!'

He rang the bell, and the bus rumbled off.

'Bother!' said Peter, disappointed. 'We might have been able to shadow him all the way home.'

'Well, I don't expect he's anything to do with the dog affair, really,' said Colin. 'We might have gone on a real wild-goose chase, and found he was just a harmless old businessman, catching a bus home.'

'Peter! Colin! Did you notice his hand?' said Jack, in a voice suddenly bubbling with excitement. 'When he put it out to take hold of the bus-rail?'

'No. Why?' said both boys at once.

'Well, he had two fingers missing, and the hand was crooked,' said Jack. 'Don't you remember Janet's report, don't you re—?'

'Gosh, yes!' said Peter. 'That man she described getting off the train from Pilberry, at the station on Saturday morning! Hat well pulled down over his eyes, he walked a bit lame, a funny hand . . .'

'And very square shoulders,' said Colin. 'It all fits. He's the same man. But wait a bit, there's nothing extraordinary about us seeing the same man as Janet saw, is there? I mean, it's only just chance, and doesn't *mean* anything.'

'No, you're right. It doesn't really mean anything,' said Jack, his excitement fading. 'It just seemed strange that's all. Perhaps we're making a mountain out of a molehill – he's just an ordinary person going home.'

They turned to walk across the square again, and passed the little alley-way that led to the yard. Someone came out of it briskly, and almost bumped into them.

It was too dark to see what the man was like, but he soon passed under a lamp-post, and something swinging from his hand caught Jack's eye.

'Look, a dog lead,' he said, in a low voice. 'But no dog! It's the same man who lives at Starling's Hotel.'

'The one I saw with the dog yesterday!' said Colin, excited. 'What's he doing here again? Has he taken another dog into that yard and pushed it down the coal-hole? Gosh! This is all very peculiar, isn't it? What *is* going on?'

They went on, keeping well behind the young man. He went round a corner, and vanished from sight. The boys went round the corner too, and then got a sudden shock.

The young man came out from a doorway as they passed and caught hold of Colin and Peter by the shoulder. He flashed a torch in their faces.

'Ha – it's you three, is it?' he said. 'Members of the famous Secret Shadowing Gang, or whatever you call yourselves! I *thought* you were following me! Look here, I took that fourth boy, what's his name, George, to his parents, and got him punished for this idiotic following of people at night. And I've a good mind to take you to the police, the three of you, and hand you over for making yourselves a nuisance by doing the same thing!'

'All right,' said Peter, at once. 'Take us to the police. We don't mind. Go on, take us!'

The young man hesitated. He evidently hadn't thought that Peter would challenge him like that. The boys stood there, scowling. Colin suddenly asked a question.

'Where's your dog?'

'What do you mean? I haven't a dog!' said the young man, angrily. 'You seem to have got dogs on your mind. You asked me that when you came to see me this afternoon.'

'Well, why the dog lead, if you haven't a dog?' said Colin, pointing to it.

'Look here, who do you think you are, asking foolish questions, interfering, following people? And what's all this about dogs? What's on your mind?'

The boys didn't answer that question. 'Are you going to take us to the police or not?' said Jack. 'We're ready, if you are. You can tell them anything you like. But we might tell them a few things too.'

'Pah!' said the young man, looking as if he would like to lash out with the dog lead at the boys. 'I've had enough of you. Clear off home, and don't let me see you again!'

Off he went with angry steps. 'Well!' said Peter, staring after him. 'He certainly didn't dare to take us to the police – but why? What a very puzzling peculiar young man!'

All these exciting happenings made it necessary to call another Secret Seven meeting as soon as possible. The members simply *must* talk over everything, and try to sort things out. So, before afternoon school on Thursday, Peter called a half-hour meeting.

'What a pity George is out of it!' said Janet. 'He would so love to hear all that's happening.'

'I don't see why we can't tell him,' said

Jack. 'He can't come to the meeting, of course, but I can't for the life of me see why we shouldn't tell him all that happens. After all, it was *his* first shadowing that began all this!'

'Well, he isn't a member,' said Peter, who liked the rules to be kept. 'We ought not to let anyone but the seven members know what we're doing. Otherwise we're not a Secret Society.'

'Woof,' said Scamper, thumping his tail on the floor of the shed. He seemed to think that he had to make some remark about everything, now that he was a proper member.

'Let's put it to the vote,' said Janet. 'I like rules being kept too, but it isn't George's fault he's out of this. I feel as if he really does still belong to us.'

So they put it to the vote, and fortunately everyone was of the same mind. George should certainly be told everything that happened. It would make up to him a little for being out of the Society. Scamper said 'Woof' so loudly when he was asked that everyone took it for 'Yes'. So it was solemnly recorded that the whole of the Secret Seven thought it right and proper to keep George up to date in the doings of the Society.

A very exciting discussion was held. Everyone wanted to talk at once, so Peter became very strict and insisted that only one person should speak at a time.

It was decided that the old man, who came out of the lighted-window building and got on the bus, was the same one that Janet had seen at the station.

'He probably lives at Pilberry,' said Janet. 'I saw him getting off the train from Pilberry, and you saw him getting on the bus for Pilberry. Though I can't see that it's at all important to know where he lives. He may not have anything to do with this affair at all.'

'That's what we said,' said Jack. 'But we feel he *might* have something to do with it, so we'll keep our eyes open for him and his doings. Your description was so good, Janet, that we all recognised him for the man you saw!'

Janet was pleased, Pam and Barbara wished heartily that they had not had giggling fits at the bus stop, but had noticed people as carefully as Janet had. Well, they would do better the next time!

The coal-hole was well and truly discussed.

'It's pretty certain that for some reason that young man takes dogs there secretly at night, and puts them through the hole,' said Colin. 'Then he leaves them. Do you suppose somebody is down there, waiting to receive them? I mean, somebody *must* look after them, surely?'

'Yes. But WHY are they taken there and hidden?' said Jack. 'That's what *I* want to know. I feel sorry for the dogs. We ought to get the RSPCA after them. It's cruel to push dogs through coal-holes and leave them there in the darkness. For all we know they have no food or drink.'

'There wouldn't be any sense in starving them,' said Peter. 'The dogs must be stolen ones. That's quite clear. We've seen one of them. You, Colin, said it was a fine bull-terrier, so it was probably a very valuable dog, and would fetch a good deal of money.'

'Yes, and the one that man must have taken last night, when we bumped into him, would have been some other kind of valuable dog, too,' said Jack. 'Gosh! Do you suppose that cellar is full of pure-bred dogs, all stolen? We'll have to do something about this!'

'Poor dogs!' said Pam. 'What happens to them down in the cellar? I do, do hope there's somebody there to see to them.'

There was a silence. Everyone was thinking the same thing. Something had got to be done about those dogs! Somehow that cellar had to be explored.

Colin, Pam and Jack began to talk loudly at the same time, and Peter rapped on the box in front of him.

'Silence! I've said you've got to talk one at a time. Has anyone any suggestions? Pam, what have you got to say?'

'Well, I've got rather a good idea,' said Pam. 'Can't we look up the Lost and Found advertisements in the newspapers, and see if many dogs are advertised as lost or stolen?'

'Yes. *Very* good idea,' said Peter, and Pam felt pleased. 'We'll do that.'

'And couldn't we go to the police station and look at the notices outside too?' asked Jack. 'They often have posters giving particulars of lost animals.'

'Excellent,' said Peter. 'Any more ideas?'

'We *must* explore that cellar,' said Colin.

'I did wonder if we should try to get into that building with the lighted window and see if its cellar led to that coal-hole – but we might get into awful trouble if we got in there. Isn't it called "Breaking in" or something?'

'Yes. We can't do that,' said Peter, firmly. 'We can't *possibly* do wrong things in order to put something right. We'll have to explore the coal-hole, but I can't see that it matters doing that. Now, we'd better make plans.'

'Everybody's got to do something!' said Jack. 'Give us our jobs, Peter, and we'll do them. Hurrah – the Secret Seven is going full speed again!'

[13]

Jobs for everyone

Peter gave each one of them a job to do. 'Pam and Barbara, hunt through every paper you can get hold of and find out if there are many valuable dogs advertised as lost or stolen,' he said.

'Yes, Peter,' said the two girls.

'And mind you do your job properly this time,' said Peter, sternly. 'Janet, you can go and look outside the police station and see if there are any notices there, and, as it's fairly near George's house, you can go and tell him all the latest news. He didn't come to school today, because he has a cough, so he'll be glad to see you.'

'Yes, Peter,' said Janet, pleased.

'And you, Colin, and you, Jack, will

come with me and Scamper to the coal-hole tonight,' said Peter, dropping his voice, and sounding suddenly serious and determined. 'Colin, bring that rope-ladder you've got. It will be just right for dropping down into the hole, it's not too long. Bring torches both of you, and wear rubber shoes.'

'Yes, Peter,' said the boys, looking and feeling very thrilled indeed. What an adventure!

'Woof-woof-woof,' said Scamper.

'He said "Yes, Peter," too!' said Janet. 'You understand every word we're saying, don't you, Scamper, darling?'

'Today's Thursday,' said Pam. 'Have you forgotten that you three boys are going to Ronnie's party, all of you? You can't do anything much today.'

'Bother! I'd forgotten that!' said Peter. 'We'll have to explore the coal-hole on Friday, then. But you girls can get on with your jobs all right. Now I think that's about all, so we'll go. We'll just be in good time for school.'

They all went out of the shed, Scamper too, wagging his tail importantly. Pam and Barbara decided to go after school to the public library, where there were many papers they could read for Lost and Found advertisements. So, much to the librarian's astonishment, they seated themselves there, with copies of the daily papers and of the local papers too, around them.

They made some interesting discoveries. 'Look, Pam,' said Barbara, pointing with her finger to two advertisements. '"Lost or stolen, pedigree greyhound." "Lost or stolen, pure-bred bull-terrier." Why, that might be the very one Colin saw! It gives names and addresses here, both in our county.'

'I've found an interesting advertisement too,' said Pam. 'See – "Lost on Monday, 16th, a beautiful pedigree Saluki. Answers to name of Sally." That's in our county too. It looks as if somebody is at work, stealing pedigree dogs!'

'Here's another,' said Barbara. '"Believed stolen, pure-bred Alsatian, well-trained, answers to name of Kip." Goodness! Suppose the boys find them all down that coal-hole!'

'What do you suppose the thief does with them?' said Pam.

'Sells them again, of course. They would be worth a lot of money,' said Barbara. 'Or they might claim the reward offered. See, there's a reward of one hundred pounds for anyone finding the Alsatian!'

'I wonder how Janet will get on, looking at the police notices!' said Pam. 'Anyway, we've done well this time. Peter can't tick us off again!'

Janet couldn't go to the police station till the following day. She gobbled down her midday dinner and raced off. She meant to look at the police notices, and then go and see George and tell him all the latest news.

There was only one notice about dogs, and that was to say that dogs found worrying sheep would be shot. Janet hoped with all her heart that Scamper would never do such a silly thing. She didn't think he would, because her father owned a lot of sheep, and Scamper was used to them. It would be so dreadful if he was shot.

She glanced at the next notice. It described a man that the police wanted to find. Janet read it with interest.

> *'John Wilfrid Pace, aged 71. Small and bent. Bald, with shaggy eyebrows and beard. Very hoarse voice. Shuffles badly when walking. Scar across the right cheek.'*

'I should know *him* all right if I saw him!' said Janet to herself, picturing a bent little man, bald and bearded, scarred on the face. 'Now I really must go and see George, or I'll be late for school.'

George was delighted to see Janet. He was perfectly all right except for a cough, but his mother was not going to let him go back to school until Monday.

'I've come to tell you all the latest news of the Secret Seven,' said Janet. 'Can anyone overhear us? We know you're not a member now, but we all voted that you should know what's going on. And there's plenty to tell you, George. It's all very, very exciting!'

So it was, and Janet told everything very well indeed. When she left George, he felt rather down in the dumps. All this going on and I'm not in it! he thought.

Then an idea came into his head. Well – why *shouldn't* I be in it? Why shouldn't I go to that coal-hole, and watch the others going down? They needn't even know I'm there! I can find it all right. Yes, I'll go. Look out, Secret Seven, I'm coming too, though you won't see me! Hurrah!

[14]

Down the coal-hole!

Ronnie's party was a good one, and the three boys and Janet enjoyed themselves thoroughly. They quite forgot the exciting affair they were mixed up in, as they played all kinds of games.

But one game reminded them of the Secret Seven doings! Ronnie's mother suddenly came in with a tray of all kinds of things. 'Now look well, everybody!' she said. 'There are twenty things here. I am going to find out which of you has the best powers of observation! Look well for one minute, and then I shall take the tray away, and you must each write down what you saw on the tray, as many as you can!'

You can guess who won that competition, Janet! She remembered all twenty, and Peter was very proud of her.

'I believe you belong to a Secret Society, Janet,' said Ronnie's mother, giving her a box of chocolates as a prize. 'You must be one of its best members!'

That reminded the three boys of the exciting thing they were to do the next night. Down the coal-hole they would go, and what would they find there?

There was no time for a proper meeting before Friday night, so Janet, Pam, and Barbara hurriedly told Peter what they had found out about lost or stolen dogs. Peter was very interested indeed, especially when he heard that most of them were from their own county.

'That rather looks as if the thieves have their quarters in the county too,' he said. 'And if so, it may be down that coal-hole! I'd like to pay back that nasty young man for getting George into trouble. I'm sure he's mixed up in this!'

It was dark about seven o'clock. The three boys and Scamper met at the end of Peter's road, and set off together. Colin had his rope-ladder, and they all had their torches. They felt very excited.

It was a dark night, and a slight drizzle was falling. The boys turned up their coat collars. They went cautiously, in case that young man should turn up again out of some corner. They didn't like him. In fact each boy was secretly afraid of him. There was something horrid about his cold eyes and thin, cruel mouth that not one of them liked.

They went down Hartley Street and across Plain Square. A bus rumbled by and a few cars.

They came near to the alley-way. 'Do you suppose that man's coming with another dog tonight?' whispered Jack. 'We'd better keep a sharp lookout in case he does. It wouldn't do for him to find us getting down the coal-hole!'

'Well, you had better keep watch while we two get down,' said Peter. 'Then as soon as we're down you can make a run for the hole and get down yourself. I only hope that man *doesn't* come – we'd be nicely trapped if he did. He's only got to pop on the lid and we're prisoners. We couldn't possibly lift up that heavy lid from inside.'

This was not at all a nice thought. They went along even more cautiously, keeping a lookout for the young man. But there was no one to be seen near the alley-way. The boys went quietly down it and came into the yard. It was pitch-dark there.

They stood and listened for a while, with Scamper silent beside them. If the man was there they might hear a slight movement, or even breathing. But they heard nothing at all. It seemed quite safe to switch on torches and go across to the coal-hole.

Peter flashed his torch round quickly. The yard was deserted, dirty as ever, and very quiet. There was not even the lighted window to see.

They moved the box that hid the coal-hole and heaved off the heavy lid, and then Peter flashed his torch down. Nothing there but blackness and dirt. Colin undid the little rope-ladder he carried and let it drop slowly down into the hole, rung by rung. Scamper watched it going down with much interest.

They peered down. Yes, it reached the bottom nicely. Colin fastened the top end carefully to a nearby stone post.

'Now, Jack, you go to the entrance of the alley and keep guard till we're down,' whispered Peter. 'Come as soon as you hear a low whistle.'

Jack sped off obediently. Colin said he would go down first. So down he climbed, rung by rung, till he came to the bottom. He flashed his torch round. He was in a big coal-cellar. His feet crunched a little as he stepped here and there, and he guessed that there was still coke or coal dust on the floor.

'I'm coming now,' whispered Peter. 'Look out, I'm bringing Scamper too!' Down he came, and soon stood beside Colin. He remembered Jack, and sent a low whistle to tell him he could come.

Soon they heard Jack's feet above, and then he came down too, grinning in delight. They were all very excited, Peter flashed his torch all round.

'Now, there must be a way out of this cellar. Look, is that a door over there?'

'Yes,' said Jack. 'That probably leads into the other cellars or basements. We'd better go cautiously – and listen hard as we go.'

'Nobody saw us go down, that's one good thing!' said Peter, thankfully.

But he was wrong. Somebody did see them go down. It is true that he could hardly make them out in the darkness, but he heard their low voices and knew what was happening! Who was it? George, of course!

George had done what he had made up his mind to do! He had found the yard with the coal-hole, and he was hiding to watch what happened. Somehow or other, Secret Seven member or not, George was going to be in on this!

[15]

Underground happenings

The three boys down in the coal-hole were now carefully opening the door they had seen. Scamper was at Peter's heels, as excited as they were. Peter wished he didn't pant quite so loudly, but Scamper couldn't help that!

The door creaked as it was opened. There was no light beyond. Peter cautiously flashed his torch on and off. A passage lay before him, leading to a few steps. A closed door was at the top of the steps.

The boys went along the passage and up the few steps and then turned the handle of the door. Would it be locked? No, it wasn't. It opened towards them, and Peter peered round the crack. Still there was darkness in front of them. He flashed his torch round.

Now they were in the main cellars that lay under the big building. They stretched here and there, low-roofed, with brick pillars standing up from floor to roof at intervals.

A noise came to Scamper's ears, and he listened, head on one side. Peter saw him listening, and listened too. But he could hear nothing. Scamper's ears were sharper than his.

They moved forward very cautiously, stopping every now and again to listen. It was very weird to be so far under a building, in the pitch darkness and loneliness of these vast cellars. They smelt strange too – musty and old and damp.

They came to another door – a wooden one – and now Scamper began to get very excited. Peter had difficulty in preventing him from barking. And then, as they opened the stout wooden door, they heard what Scamper heard!

It was the noise of whining dogs! Scamper whined too when he heard, and wanted to dash through the door. Then came a barking and a yapping. Then more whining.

'There *are* dogs shut up here,' whispered Peter. 'We were right. Go carefully now, for goodness' sake.'

They came to a long, narrow cellar, where a faint light glowed from a glass bulb. On one side was a wooden bench, on which cages were set. In them were five or six dogs, their eyes gleaming red in the faint light.

Nobody was there with the dogs. They gazed warily and snarled as the three boys came quietly near, but when Scamper gave an excited, friendly whine, they whined too, pawing at their cages in excitement.

'They've got water and food,' whispered Peter. 'Oh, look, there's the lovely car-sick poodle we saw in that car, Jack, do you remember? We saw it when we were doing a bit of practice, hiding by the road in a spyhole, watching people go by. I'm sure it's the same poodle.'

'Yes. It is,' said Jack. 'Colin, there's a bull-terrier, see? He's the same one you saw with that young man, I suppose?'

Colin nodded. He was very fond of dogs, and he was already making friends with these, allowing them to lick his hand through the wires of the cages.

'There's a greyhound, and a magnificent Alsatian!' said Peter. 'I bet those are the ones the girls read about in the papers as lost or stolen. And here's a Dalmatian – hallo, Spots! You're a beauty, aren't you?'

The dogs were now all very friendly to the boys, partly because they had a dog with them who was friendly too. Peter stood and looked at the dogs, wondering what to do next.

'Should we set them free from their cages, tie them together with rope and see if we can get them out of the coal-hole?' he said.

'Don't be silly!' said Colin. 'They'd never go up the rope-ladder – and I bet they'd begin to fight if we set them free.'

'Listen, somebody's coming!' said Jack, suddenly, and Scamper gave a warning growl. The boys went into the shadows and waited.

They saw an old bent man shuffling along, carrying a lantern. His head shone in the faint radiance of the electric light above, for he was quite bald. He had a small dog with him, a mongrel of some kind, and he talked to it as he came in a curious, hoarse voice like a creaking gate!

'Come on, Tinks. We'll see if all the lords and ladies are all right. They don't think nothing of the likes of you and me, but we don't care, do we?'

The little dog trotted beside him, and they

came to the cages. The old man went on talking in his creaking voice, staring at the caged dogs.

'Well, my high-and-mighty ones, my lords and ladies, you're worse off than little Tinks here. You've lost your own masters, but he's got his. You may be worth your weight in gold, for all I know, but you'd give all you've got for a nice long walk, wouldn't you? Well, Tinks goes for two each day. Tell 'em, Tinks, tell 'em.'

But Tinks was not listening. He had smelt strange smells, the smells of the three boys and the golden spaniel, Scamper! In a moment he was over beside them, barking madly.

The old man held up his lantern and peered at them. 'What, more visitors?' he creaked. 'Come to see the lords and ladies, have you? Wait now, you're only lads!'

Peter came out from the shadows with Jack and Colin. He didn't feel at all afraid of this strange old man.

'Where did these dogs come from?' he said. 'Who brought them here? Who do they belong to? What are you doing with them?'

The old man gave him a helpless look.

'Them dogs, why, they comes and they goes,' he said. 'They comes and they goes. They comes in at that hole and—'

But whatever he said next was quite drowned by a sudden yelping and barking by the dogs. They had heard somebody else coming. Who was it this time?

''Ere comes the Guvnor,' said the old man, and chuckled drily. 'Now you'll be in trouble. Likely he'll lock you up in them cages!'

[16]

Unpleasant surprises

Somebody came up out of the shadows very suddenly and quietly. The boys swung round at his voice.

'And what are *you* doing here?'

It was the tall, stooping man they had seen coming out of the building and getting on the bus! Yes, hat well pulled down, squared shoulders, odd hand! They couldn't see his face even now, under the shade of his black hat.

The boys, taken by surprise, didn't know what to say. The man suddenly opened a nearby cage, and spoke loudly.

'Guard them, Kip.'

The enormous Alsatian leapt out, went to the boys and glared at them, snarling and showing his teeth. Scamper shrank back, afraid. The boys didn't like it at all, either. They didn't dare to move a step.

The man laughed. 'That's right. Keep still. See my hand with two fingers off? Well, that's what an Alsatian did to me when I moved while he was guarding me!'

The boys said nothing. Peter felt wild with himself. They had thought themselves so clever, getting down to explore these cellars and see what they could find, and now they were trapped, and guarded by the fiercest Alsatian he had ever seen. He hoped and hoped that Scamper would not do anything silly. Kip would gobble him up in a mouthful.

The man fired questions at them. 'How did you come here? What for? Does anyone know you are here? Do you know the kind of things that happen to boys who poke their noses into things that are no concern of theirs? You don't? Then you soon will!'

He gave a sudden sharp order to the bald old man, who was muttering to himself in his creaking voice. 'Got your keys? Then lock these boys up in the cages. Kip, bring them here.'

Kip rounded up the boys as if they had been sheep, and hustled them in front of the man. Then one by one the Alsatian propelled each of them into a cage, snarling if they resisted. The old bald man locked them in, chortling to himself. Colin saw there was a scar across his face as the man looked up at him. There was no doubt about it, he was the old man that Janet had read about in the police notice! But not one of them could tell the police that the fellow was here, because they were all well and truly locked up.

The dogs were roaming about, growling and uneasy. The stooping man had them under control, though, and one sharp word from him was obeyed at once by any dog. He stood in front of the cages mockingly.

Scamper was not in a cage, but crouched outside Peter's, frightened and puzzled.

'I'm going now,' said the tall man to the little bald fellow. 'I'm taking the dogs in the car. You won't see me again. It's too dangerous here now. You don't need to know anything if anyone comes asking questions. Just play the idiot – that should be easy for you!'

'I'm afraid of the police,' creaked the old man.

'Well, hide away in the cellars,' said the other. 'It's a warren of a place. No one will ever find you. Let these kids out in twenty-four hours' time. I'll be well away by then, so it doesn't matter what kind of tale they tell! They don't know anything, anyway.'

'We do!' said Peter, boldly. 'We know that all these dogs are stolen. We know that this bald man is wanted by the police. We know the young man who brings the dogs here for you! We know you use the building above this cellar for your headquarters. We know—'

The tall man limped over to Peter's cage. For one moment the boy saw his furious, gleaming eyes and was afraid. Scamper thought he was about to harm Peter, and he flew at him and bit him hard on the ankle!

The man gave an exclamation and kicked out at Scamper. He caught him in the mouth, and the dog fled away yelping, and was lost in the shadows.

Then the man was gone, and with him went the dogs, cowed and obedient. He obviously had some extraordinary control over them – perhaps he had been a dog trainer, Peter thought. The old bald man laughed hoarsely at the frightened faces of the three boys in the cages, and his little mongrel dog sat down beside him with his mouth open as if he was laughing too.

'Boys! I don't like boys! Nasty tormenting creatures. I always said they ought to be shut up in cages!' He gave a creaking laugh. 'And now here you are, locked in my cages, and nobody knows where you are. Shall I tell you something, young sirs? If the police come after me and take me, I'll not tell them about you. I'll say to myself, "What, you'll take poor old John Pace and shut him up? Aha! Then I won't tell you about those boys!"'

He went off into a cackle of laughter, and then set off with his little mongrel at his heels. The boys were silent for a moment and then Peter spoke.

'We're properly caught. Goodness knows how long we'll be in this dark, horrible, smelly place. I wonder where Scamper's gone. He can't get up that rope-ladder by himself, or he'd go home and get help. I hope he's not hurt.'

'Sh! Listen! There's somebody else coming!' said Colin. 'I heard something, I'm sure. Gosh! I hope it's not that horrible young man. It would be just our luck if he came along with another dog for the other man!'

There was a pattering noise as well as cautious footsteps. Was it that young man and a dog? The three boys held their breath as the footsteps came nearer and nearer. Then a torch suddenly flashed out on the cages!

[17]

Good old George!

A familiar voice came to the three boys' ears. 'Peter! Colin! Jack! Whatever are you doing in those cages?'

'Why, it's George! George, is it really you?' cried Peter, joyfully. 'And Scamper! Is Scamper hurt?'

'No. But what on earth has happened?' said George, in the greatest amazement, as he gazed at the boys in the cages.

'How did *you* get in here?' demanded Jack. 'I was never so surprised in all my life as when I heard your voice.'

'I knew you were coming here tonight, because Janet told me,' explained George. 'And I thought I'd come too, even though I didn't belong to the Secret Seven any more.

I thought I'd just watch. I saw you go down, and gosh! I did want to join you. I was hiding in that yard.'

'Well, I never!' said Peter. 'What made you come down into the cellars, then?'

'I waited ages for you to come back, and you didn't,' said George. 'And then I suddenly heard old Scamper whining like anything down in the hole. So I hopped out of my hiding-place and went down the ladder to him. That's all. But WHY are you in those cages? Can't you get out?'

'No,' groaned Peter. 'It's too long a story to tell you, George. You must go and get the police. Wait, though, look round first and see if that old man has hung the cage keys anywhere!'

George flashed his torch here and there, and gave a sudden exclamation.

'Yes, here are some keys, on this nail. I'll try them in the padlocks.'

He tried first one and then another in the

padlock on Peter's cage door, and there was a sudden click!

'Oh good!' said Peter, as the lock opened. He pushed open the cage door. Soon the others were out too. They were most relieved.

'Now quick, we'll get the police,' said Peter. 'Come on, Scamper, old thing. Fancy you going and whining to George like that! I suppose you knew he was hiding in that yard, though *we* didn't!'

They hurried through the cellars, and came to the coal-hole. Up the rope-ladder they went. They pulled up the ladder and then picked their way through the yard, their hearts beating quickly. Scamper was very pleased with himself indeed. He felt that he had been a first-class member of the Secret Seven!

The four boys and the dog caused quite a sensation at the police station, arriving dirty and full of excitement. The police sergeant was there. He knew them, and was far more willing to listen to their extraordinary story than the old policemen would have been.

They poured it out, and the sergeant called a most interested policeman to take down notes.

The story went on and on, taken up first by one boy, then another. 'Stolen dogs – the coal-hole – the young man and the dog that vanished – the cellars below – the strange bald caretaker who looked after the dogs – yes, he's the man you've got a notice about outside the police station. The tall, stooping man – yes, he's got away. He's taken the dogs – in a car, he said.'

'I bet he's taken them in that car we saw the sick poodle in the other day!' said Peter, suddenly. 'I bet he has. Wait – I've got the number here. If you could find that car, sir, you'd probably find all the dogs *and* that man too! Gosh! I can't find the bit of paper I wrote down the number on.' He fumbled anxiously in all his pockets but the paper was not there.

'Think of the number. Try hard!' urged the sergeant. 'This is important. If we get that number, we can send out details, and the car will be stopped in a few minutes, no matter where it is. Think.'

'I know the *number*,' groaned Peter. 'It was 188. But what were the letters?'

'I know! Pretty Sick Dog!' cried Jack, suddenly remembering.

The sergeant looked astonished. 'Pretty Sick Dog?' he said. 'I don't follow.'

'PSD,' grinned Jack. 'The dog was sick, so we said the car letters must stand for Pretty Sick Dog – see? That's it – PSD 188.'

'Telephone that number to the patrol cars,' said the sergeant to the policeman. 'Quick now! We'll get him yet. My word, we've been after these dog stealers for months. That fellow's a wonder at getting any dog to come to him, then he pops it into his car and away it goes. He hands it to somebody else, who passes it on again—'

'Yes, they go to the young man who lives at Starling's Hotel!' said Peter. 'We know he put a dog down the coal-hole to the old caretaker with the bald head and scar. You could get that young man too, Sergeant. He doesn't know about the happenings to-night! And you can get the caretaker as well. You've only to send men down the coal-hole into the cellar and up into the building above.'

The sergeant stared at Peter in awe. 'I haven't time to ask you how you know all these remarkable things,' he said. 'Car numbers – young men at Starling's – stolen dogs and their hiding-place – wanted men – I just haven't time. I can't understand it.'

'Oh, well, we belong to the best Secret Society in the world, you know,' said Peter, unable to help boasting. 'We are always on the lookout for things to happen. Actually, we weren't *really* on the lookout this time. We rather *made* them happen, I think.'

The sergeant laughed. 'Well, make a few more happen. Now you'd better get home. It's late. I'll come and see you tomorrow. So long, and many, many thanks!'

[18]

The jigsaw is finished

Eight worried and amazed fathers and mothers heard the strange story of the stolen dogs when the four boys at last got home, very late, and full of excitement. Janet heard Peter come in, and flew downstairs from her bed, anxious to hear everything.

'What! You found the dogs in cages! And oh, how extraordinary that the man I read about on that police notice was there! Oh, goodness, were you really locked up in the dog-cages? And did Scamper, dear, darling, brave old Scamper, go and fetch George to your rescue? Scamper, you are one of the very, very best Secret Seven members!'

'Woof!' said Scamper, proudly, and sat up very straight.

Janet laughed at the Pretty Sick Dog business. So did everybody. It struck them as very funny. The whole adventure seemed rather extraordinary now it was over. It was a curious mystery, a strange little adventure, that had really grown out of the 'job' and 'practices' that Peter had set all the members to do.

'In fact, we each had one bit of a jigsaw puzzle, and when we found they fitted together, we saw what the picture was!' said Peter. 'We each did our bit, even old George.'

Next morning there was a Secret Seven meeting, of course, and will you believe it, George was there too, beaming all over his face.

'I say, can I come in?' he said, when he arrived, and banged on the door. 'Oh, the password, it's still "Beware", isn't it? It was a very good one for this adventure, wasn't it? We all had to "Beware" like anything. I guessed you'd have a Secret Seven meeting this morning, so I've come too. My father says I can be a member again if you'll have me!'

'Oh, George!' cried everyone in delight, and Peter dragged him in at once. 'Did he really? Why? Because we've done such a good job again, and you helped?'

'Yes. You see, the Inspector and the sergeant both came to ask me a few questions, and they told Dad and Mother that all the Secret Seven were quite remarkable people, and Dad never said a word about having had me turned out! And after the policemen had gone, Dad said "All right, George. I give in. You can belong again. You can go and tell the Secret Seven to make you a member again." So here I am.'

'We solemnly make you a member, George,' said Janet in delight. 'Scamper, we told you you were only temporary, didn't we? So you won't mind George taking your place. But you were very, very good as a member, Scamper. Wasn't he, everybody?'

They all agreed heartily, and Scamper looked pleased and surprised to have so many pats and kind words. He gave a little whine as if to say 'Well, what about a biscuit too?'

And Janet, always ready to understand his smallest whine, at once produced a big biscuit from a tin! 'You deserve it,' she said. 'If you hadn't gone to fetch George to the rescue last night, Peter and Colin and Jack would still be locked up in the dog-cages!'

'Gosh! So we would,' said Peter. 'Hallo, who's this coming?'

The big kindly face of the Inspector looked through the little window, with the sergeant alongside.

'We don't know the password,' said the Inspector, sorrowfully. 'Or we'd say it and come in.'

'It's "Beware"!' said Peter grinning, and flung open the door. 'We'll soon have to choose a new one, so it doesn't matter telling you.'

'Have you got any news?' asked Colin eagerly.

'Oh yes, that's why we came to find you,' said the Inspector. 'We thought you ought to know the results of the good work done by the remarkable Society you belong to!'

'Oh good – tell us!' said Janet.

'Well, we got the PSD 188 car,' said the Inspector. 'Got it at Pilberry.'

'Oh yes, why didn't we think of that?' said Peter. 'We *thought* that fellow lived at Pilberry!'

'Bless us, did you now?' said the Inspector. 'I'm beginning to wonder if there's anything you *don't* know! Well, we got the car, and the dogs. The man has got a shop there, with two or three garages. He'd put the dogs into one of the garages. Goodness knows how many dogs he's stolen and sold. Ah, well PSD stood for Pretty Sick Driver by the time we'd told him all we knew about him!'

'And we also got the old caretaker fellow,' said the sergeant. 'He's a poor old stick, though, a bit feeble-minded, but clever enough to help a dog-stealer, it seems! We wondered where he had gone to earth, and there he was, in this town, under our very noses!'

'We got the young man, too, at Starling's,' said the Inspector. 'He's a bad lot. He and the other man ran this dog-stealing business between them, quite cleverly too. Covered their tracks well all the time, and bamboozled us nicely. But they couldn't bamboozle the Secret Seven, could they?'

he added, getting up. 'Well, we must be off. Thanks, all of you. I wish there were more children like you, you're a grand lot to have in our town!'

The two big policemen went out, and the children shut the door and grinned happily at one another.

'Bamboozle,' said Colin, slowly. 'Bamboozle, that would be a fine word for our next password. What about it? Bamboozle, nobody would ever guess that, so long as Jack doesn't write it down for Susie to see!'

'Don't tease him,' said Janet. 'I do feel so happy, what with George back again, and all! What about a round of ice-creams? I've got my Saturday money today. I'll treat you all. Yes, and you too, Scamper darling! If anyone has earned an ice-cream, *you* have!'

'WOOF!' said Scamper, thoroughly agreeing, thumping his tail so hard on the floor that it raised quite a dust. 'WOOF!'

So there go the Secret Seven out into the sunshine, Scamper too. I do really think they're a fine Secret Society, don't you? And I can't help wondering whatever they will be up to next!

GOOD WORK, SECRET SEVEN

[1]

Secret Seven meeting

'When are the Secret Seven going to have their next meeting?' said Susie to her brother Jack.

'That's nothing to do with *you*!' said Jack. 'You don't belong to it, and what's more, you never will!'

'Goodness! *I* don't want to belong to it!' said Susie, putting on a very surprised voice. 'If I want to belong to a secret society I can always get one of my own. I did once before, and it was a better one than yours.'

'Don't be silly,' said Jack. 'Our Secret Seven is the best in the world. Why, just think of the things we've done and the adventures we've had! I bet we'll have another one soon.'

'I bet you won't,' said Susie, annoyingly. 'You've been meeting in that shed at the bottom of Peter and Janet's garden for weeks now, and there isn't even the *smell* of a mystery!'

'Well, mysteries don't grow on trees, nor do adventures,' said Jack. 'They just happen all in a minute. Anyway, I'm not going to talk about the Secret Seven any more, and you needn't think you'll get anything out of me, because you won't, Susie. And please go out of my room and let me get on with this book.'

'I know your latest password,' said Susie, half-way through the door.

'You do *not*!' said Jack, quite fiercely. 'I haven't mentioned it, and I haven't even written it down so that I won't forget it. You're a story-teller, Susie.'

'I'm not! I'm just telling you so as to warn you to choose a *new* password!' said Susie, and slid out of the door.

Jack stared after her. What an *annoying* sister she was! *Did* she know the password? No, she *couldn't* know it, possibly!

It was true what Susie had said. The Secret Seven had been meeting for weeks, and absolutely nothing had turned up. Certainly the Seven had plenty of fun together, but after having so many exciting adventures it was a bit dull just to go on playing games and talking.

Jack looked in his notebook. When was the next meeting? Tomorrow night, in Peter's shed. Well, that would be quite exciting, because all the members had been told to bring any old clothes they could find. They were going to make the Guy for their bonfire at the next meeting. It would be fun seeing what everyone had brought.

Bonfire Night was next week. Jack got up and rummaged in one of his drawers. Ah, there was his money which he kept in an old tin. Jack counted it carefully. There was just enough to buy a firework called a Humdinger. Jack was sure none of the other members of the Secret Seven would have one of those.

'Fizzzzz – whoooosh—'

'Jack! What in the world are you doing? Are you ill?' called an anxious voice, and his mother's head came round the door.

'No, Mother, I'm all right,' said Jack. 'I was thinking of a Humdinger on Bonfire Night and the noise it will make.'

'Humdinger? Whatever's that?' asked his mother.

'It's a big firework that makes lots of bangs and whooshes. I've saved up enough money to get one. Please will you ask Daddy to buy me one when he goes to do the shopping for Bonfire Night?'

'Give your father the money and he'll get you one,' said his mother. 'Oh, Jack, how untidy your bedroom is. Do tidy it up!'

'I was *just* tidying it,' said Jack to his mother. 'Hey, could you let me have some of those chocolate biscuits out of the tin? We're having a Secret Seven meeting tomorrow night.'

'Very well. Take seven,' said his mother.

'Eight, you mean,' called Jack, as she went out of the room. '*Mother*! Eight, I want. You've forgotten Scamper.'

'Goodness! Well, if you *must* waste good chocolate biscuits on a dog, take eight,' called his mother.

Good, thought Jack. We've all got to take something nice to eat tomorrow night, for the meeting. Choc biscuits will be great! Now, what was the password? Guy Fawkes, wasn't it? Or was that last time's? No, that's the one. Guy Fawkes – and a jolly good password, seeing that Bonfire Night is soon coming! Why does Susie say she knows it? She doesn't!

The meeting was for half-past five, in Peter's shed, and all the Secret Seven meant to be there. Just before the half-hour five children began to file in at Peter's gate and make their way down the garden to the shed where the meetings were held.

The shed door was shut, but a light shone from inside. On the door were the letters

S.S., put there by Peter. It was dark, and one by one torches shone on the door as the members arrived.

Rat-tat!

'Password, please!' That was Peter's voice inside.

'Guy Fawkes!' answered the members one by one.

Pamela was first. Then came Jack, hurrying in case he was late. Then George, carrying a bag of rosy apples as his share of the food. Then Barbara, wondering if the password was Guy Fawkes or Bonfire Night. Oh dear!

Rat-tat! She knocked at the door.

'Password!'

'Er – Bonfire Night,' said Barbara.

The door remained shut, and there was a dead silence inside. Barbara gave a little giggle.

'All right. I know it! Guy Fawkes!'

The door opened and she went in. Everyone was there except Colin.

'He's late,' said Peter. 'Bother him! Look, what a spread we've got tonight!'

The shed was warm and cosy inside. It was lit by two candles, and there was a small oil-stove at the back. On a table made of a box was spread the food the members had brought.

'Apples. Ginger buns. Doughnuts. Peppermint rock, and what's in this bag? Oh yes, hazelnuts from your garden, Pam. *And* you've remembered to bring nutcrackers too. Good. And I've brought orangeade. What a feast!' said Peter.

'I wish Colin would hurry up,' said Janet. 'Oh, here he is!'

There was the sound of running feet and somebody banged at the door. Rat-tat!

'Password!' yelled everyone.

'Guy Fawkes!' answered a voice, and Peter opened the door.

Well, would you believe it! It was *Susie* outside, grinning all over her cheeky face. *Susie*!

[2]

That awful Susie!

'Susie!' cried Jack, springing up in a rage. 'How dare you! You – you – you . . .'

He caught hold of his sister and held her tight. She laughed at him.

'It's all right; I just wanted to give your high-and-mighty members a shock. Aha! I know your password, see?'

'How did you know it?' demanded Peter. 'Let her go, Jack. We'll turn her out in a minute. How did you know the password, Susie?'

'I got it from Jack, of course,' said Susie, most surprisingly.

Everyone stared at poor Jack, who went as red as a beetroot. He glared at Susie.

'You're a wicked story-teller! I never told you the password and I didn't even write it down, in case you found it. How *did* you know it? Were you listening in the bushes round the shed? Did you hear us say the password as we came in?'

'No. If I had, Scamper would have barked,' said Susie, which was quite true. 'I tell you, Jack, I heard you say it yourself. You were talking in your sleep last night and you kept yelling out "Guy Fawkes! Let me in! Guy Fawkes!" So I guessed you were trying to get into the meeting in your sleep and were yelling out the password.'

Jack groaned. 'I do talk in my sleep, but who would have thought I'd yell out the password? I'll keep my bedroom door shut in future. I'm sorry, Peter. What are we going to do with Susie? She ought to be punished for bursting in on our secret meeting like this!'

'Well, we've nothing important to discuss, so we'll make Susie sit in that corner over there, and we'll have our feast, and not offer her a single thing,' said Peter, firmly.

'I'm tired of Susie, always trying to upset our Society. Pam and Barbara, sit her down over there.'

Everyone was so very cross with Susie that she began to feel upset. 'It was only a joke,' she said. 'Anyway, your meetings are silly. You go on and on having them and nothing happens at all. Let me go.'

'Well, promise on your honour you'll never try to trick us again or upset our meetings?' said Peter, sternly.

'No. I won't promise,' said Susie. 'And I shan't sit still in this corner, and I shan't keep quiet. You're to let me go.'

'Certainly not,' began Peter. 'You forced yourself in, and you can jolly well stop and see us eating all—'

He stopped very suddenly as he heard the sound of panting breath, and running feet coming down the garden path.

'It's Colin!' said Janet.

Tnere was a loud rat-tat at the door, and

the password. 'Guy Fawkes! Quick, open the door.'

The door was opened and Colin came in, blinking at the sudden light, after the darkness outside.

'Hey, I've had an adventure! It might be something for the Secret Seven. Listen!'

'Wait! Turn Susie out first!' said Peter.

Colin stared in surprise at seeing Susie there. She gave a sudden giggle, and Jack scowled at her.

'What's she doing here, anyway?' asked Colin, most astonished, as he watched Susie being hustled out of the shed.

The door was slammed and locked. Scamper, the golden spaniel who belonged to Peter and Janet, barked loudly. He hadn't at all approved of Susie being in his shed. He knew she wasn't a member!

'Tell you about Susie later,' said Peter. 'Now, Colin, what's all this about? Why are you late, and what's happened? And for goodness' sake, let's all talk quietly, because Susie is sure to be listening at the door!'

'I'll jolly well see that she isn't,' said Jack, getting up, but Peter pulled him back.

'Sit down! Don't you know it's just what Susie would like, to be chased all over the garden in the dark, spoiling our feast and our meeting and everything! Let her listen at the door if she wants to. She won't hear a word if we whisper. Be quiet, Scamper! I can't hear myself speak with you barking at the top of your voice. Can't *you* whisper too?'

Scamper couldn't. He stopped barking and lay down with his back to Peter, looking rather hurt. But he soon turned himself round again when Colin began his tale.

'I was coming along to the meeting, shining my torch as I came, and when I got to the corner of Beeches Lane, I heard somebody in the clump of bushes there. You know there's quite a little thicket at that corner. There was a lot of whispering going on, and then suddenly I heard a yell and a groan . . .'

'Gosh!' said Janet, startled.

'And somebody fell heavily. I shone my torch at the bushes, but someone knocked it out of my hand,' went on Colin. 'Then I heard the sound of running feet. I went to pick up my torch, which was still shining brightly on the ground, but by the time I shone it into the bushes again, nobody was there!'

'You were really brave to pick it up and look into the bushes,' said Peter. 'What was going on, do you think?'

'I can't imagine, except that there was a quarrel of some sort,' said Colin. 'That isn't all, though. Look what I found in the bushes.'

The Secret Seven were now so excited that they had quite forgotten about whispering. They had raised their voices, and not one of them remembered that Susie might be outside. Scamper gave a little warning growl, but nobody paid any attention.

Colin was holding out a worn and battered notebook, with an elastic band round it. 'I've had a quick look inside,' he said, 'and it might be important. A lot of it is in code, I can't read it, and there's a lot of nonsense too. At least it sounds like nonsense, but I expect it's part of a code. Look!'

They all looked. Everyone began to feel excited. Peter turned the pages and came to a list written down one page. 'Look!' he said. 'Here's a list that might be a record of stolen goods. Listen . . . silver candlesticks, three-branches, cigarette box with initials A.G.B., four silver cups, engraved—'

Jack sprang up. 'I know what all that is! My father read the list out at breakfast this morning. It was in the paper. It's a list of the things stolen from the famous cricketer, Bedwall, last night. Whew! Do you suppose we're on to something, Peter?'

[3]

Exciting plans

The Secret Seven were so thrilled that their excitement made Scamper begin to bark again. He just couldn't help it when he heard them all talking at once. He waved his plumy tail and pawed at Peter, who took no notice at all.

'It must be a notebook kept by one of the thieves, a list of things he stole!'

'What else does it say? I wish we could understand all this stuff in secret code. Wait, look, here's a note scribbled right across this page! See what it says?'

' "Gang meet in old workmen's shed, back of Lane's garage," ' read Peter. ' "5 p.m. Wednesday." Whew! That's tomorrow. Gosh, we *are* on to something.'

Everyone began to talk excitedly again,

and Scamper thought it was a very good time to sample a chocolate biscuit and perhaps a ginger bun. Before he did so he ran to the door and sniffed.

Yes. Susie was outside. Scamper could smell her. He growled a little, but as no one took any notice, and he was afraid to bark again, he went back to the good things on the little box-table.

'What are we going to do about this? Tell the police?' asked Colin, who felt most important at bringing all this exciting news to the Seven.

'No. I'll tell you what we'll do,' said Peter. 'We'll creep round to that old shed tomorrow night ourselves, and as soon as we see the gang is safely there, one of us can rush round to the police station, while the rest keep guard on the shed.'

It was decided that that would be a good, sensible and exciting thing to do. Pam gave a huge sigh.

'Excitement makes me feel so hungry. Can't we start on the buns and things? Oh, Scamper, you've been helping yourself! Thief-dog!'

'Scamper! Have you really been taking things?' said Peter, shocked. 'Go into the corner.'

'He's only taken a choc biscuit and a ginger bun,' said Jack, counting everything quickly. 'There should be eight of each thing, but there are only seven of the biscuits and the buns. So really he's only eaten what we brought for *him*, the eighth person.'

'Well, he shouldn't begin before we do,' said Peter. 'He ought to know his manners. Corner, Scamper!'

Poor Scamper retired to the corner, licking his lips for stray chocolate crumbs. He looked so woe-begone that everyone felt extremely sorry for him.

The clothes brought by the Secret Seven for the Guy were quite forgotten. The evening's events were much too exciting even to think about the Guy. The Seven made their plans as they ate.

'Gosh, we forgot all about Susie!' said Peter, suddenly. 'We've been yelling out our plans at the tops of our voices. Bother! Scamper, see if Susie is at the door!'

Scamper obediently ran to the door and sniffed. No, Susie was no longer there. He came back and sat down by Peter, putting his lovely golden head on the boy's knee, hoping for a forgiving pat.

'Oh, so she's not there. You'd have growled if she had been, wouldn't you, Scamper?' said Peter, stroking the dog's silky head and fondling his long ears. 'Well, Susie will be most astonished to hear about our adventure when it's over – serve her right for laughing at us and trying to spoil our meeting!'

It was arranged that all the Seven should go quietly to Lane's garage the next night, after tea. Colin knew Larry, a boy who helped at the garage, and it would be quite easy for the Seven to talk to him and admire the cars until it was time to look about for the workmen's shed behind the garage. Then what would happen? A little thrill of excitement ran all the way up Peter's back when he thought of it.

The Secret Seven are on the move again! he thought. What a good thing, after all these dull weeks when nothing happened!

It seemed a long time till the next afternoon. Everyone at the schools the Secret Seven went to was sure that something was up. The Seven wore their badges, and a lot of whispering went on. All the members looked important and serious.

Susie was very annoying. She kept looking at Pam, Janet and Barbara, who were in her class, and giggling. Whenever she passed them she whispered in their ear:

'Guy Fawkes! Guy Fawkes!'

This was very annoying because it was

still the password of the Secret Seven! They had completely forgotten to change it the night before, in the excitement of making plans. Now Susie still knew it. They must change it as quickly as they could.

At four o'clock all the Secret Seven rushed home early to tea, so that they could be off again immediately to the garage. They were to meet Colin there at a quarter to five.

All their mothers were astonished to see how quickly the children gobbled their teas that afternoon, but luckily nobody was made to stop at home afterwards. One by one they made their way to the garage. Scamper was left behind, in case he barked at an awkward moment.

Everyone was at the garage at a quarter to five. Only fifteen minutes more! Now, where was Larry? They must talk to him for a little while, and then creep round to the shed at the back. How exciting!

[4]

A dreadful shock

Colin was already looking for Larry, the boy he knew who helped at the garage. Ah, there he was, washing a car over in the corner. Colin went over to him, and the other six followed.

'Good evening,' said Larry, grinning at the Seven. He had a shock of fair hair and a very dirty face and twinkling eyes. 'Come to help me?'

'I wish we were allowed to,' said Colin. 'I'd love to mess about with cars. Larry, can we have a look at the ones you've got in the garage now?'

'Yes, so long as you don't open the doors,' said the lad, splashing the water very near Colin's feet.

The Seven divided up and went to look at the cars near the doorway and wide windows, so that they could keep an eye on anyone passing. They might see the 'gang', whoever they were.

'Look! Doesn't *he* look as if he might be one of the gang?' whispered Barbara, nudging Jack as a man went by.

Jack glanced at him.

'Idiot!' he said. 'That's my headmaster. Good thing he didn't hear you! Still, he does look a bit grim!'

'It's five to five,' said George in a low voice. 'I think we'd better go round to the shed soon, Peter.'

'Not yet,' said Peter. 'We don't want to be there when the men arrive. Seen anyone likely to belong to the gang?'

'Not really,' said George. 'Everybody looks rather *ordinary*. But then, the gang might look ordinary too. Gosh, I *am* beginning to feel excited!'

A little later, when the garage clock said a minute past five, Peter gave the signal to move. They all said goodbye to Larry, who playfully splashed hose-water round their ankles as they ran out.

'Bother him, my socks are soaked,' said Jack. 'Do we go down this alley-way, Peter?'

'Yes. I'll go first, and if all's clear I'll give a low whistle,' said Peter.

He went down the alley in the darkness, holding his torch, but not putting it on. He came to the yard behind the garage, where the workmen's shed was.

He stopped in delight. There was a light in it! The gang *were* in there, then! My word, if only they could catch the whole lot at once.

Peter gave a low whistle, and the others trooped down the alley to him. They all wore rubber-soled shoes, and made no noise at all. Their hearts beat fast and

Barbara felt out of breath, hers thumped so hard. They all stared at the little shed, with the dim light shining from its one small window.

'They must be there,' whispered Jack. 'Let's creep up and see if we can peep in at the window.'

They crept noiselessly up to the shed. The window was high up and Peter had to put a few bricks on top of one another to stand on, so that he could reach the window.

He stepped down and whispered to the others: 'They're there. I can't see them, but I can hear them. Shall we get the police straight away, do you think?'

'Well, I'd like to be sure it isn't just *workmen* inside,' said Jack. 'They might be having their tea there or something, you know. Workmen do have a lot of meals, and that shed's pretty cosy, I should think.'

'What are we to do, then? We can't knock on the door and say, "Are you workmen or do you belong to the gang?"' said Peter.

A loud bang came suddenly from the shed and made everyone jump. Barbara clutched at George and made him jump again.

'Was that a gun?' she said. 'They're not shooting, are they?'

'*Don't* grab me like that!' said George, in a fierce whisper. 'You nearly made me yell out. How do I know if it's shooting?'

Another loud bang came, and the Seven once more jumped violently, Peter was puzzled. What was happening in that shed? He suddenly saw that there was a keyhole. Perhaps if he bent down and looked through that he would be able to see what was happening inside.

So he bent down and squinted through the keyhole, and sure enough, he got quite a view, though a narrow one, of the inside of the candle-lit shed.

What he saw filled him with such astonishment that he let out a loud exclamation. He couldn't believe his eyes. He simply couldn't!

'What is it, what is it?' cried Pam, quite forgetting to speak in a whisper. 'Are they shooting? Let *me* look!'

She dragged Peter away and put her eye to the keyhole, and she, too, gave a squeal. Then, to the amazement of all the others but Peter, she began to kick and bang at the locked door! She shouted loudly:

'It's *Susie* in there, Susie and some others! I can see her grinning like anything, and they've got big paper bags to pop. That's what made the bangs. It's Susie; it's all a trick; it's SUSIE!'

So it was. Susie, with Jim and Doris and Ronnie, and now they were rolling over the floor, squealing with laughter. Oh, what a *wonderful* trick they had played on the Secret Seven!

[5]

A victory for Susie

The Secret Seven were so angry that they hardly knew what to do. So it was Susie and her friends who had planned all this! While Susie had been boldly giving the password and forcing her way into their meeting the night before, her friends were pretending to scuffle in the bushes to stop Colin and make him think something really serious was going on!

'They took me in properly,' groaned Colin. 'I really thought it was men scuffling there, and I was so pleased to find that notebook when they had run off! It was too dark to spot that they weren't men, of course.'

'No wonder Susie giggled all the time she

was in our shed, and laughed when Colin rushed in to tell us of his adventure!' said Janet. 'Horrid, tiresome girl!'

'She's the worst sister possible,' said Jack, gloomily. 'Fancy putting that list of stolen things in the notebook, of course, *she* had heard my father read them out at breakfast-time too. Bother Susie!'

George kicked at the shed door. From the inside came the sound of shrieks of delighted laughter, and some enormous guffaws from Jim, who, like Doris, was rolling about from side to side, holding his aching sides. Oh, what a joke! Oh, to think they had brought the stuck-up Secret Seven all the way to this shed, just to see *them*!

'You just wait till you unlock the door and come out!' called Jack. 'You just wait! I'll pull your hair till you squeal, Susie. I'm ashamed of you!'

More squeals of laughter, and a loud,

'Ho, ho, ho,' from Jim again. It really was maddening.

'There's seven of us, and only four of you,' cried Colin, warningly. 'And we'll wait here till you come out, see? You hadn't thought of that, had you?'

'Oh yes, we had,' called Susie. 'But you'll let us go free – you see if you don't.'

'We shan't!' said Jack, furiously. 'Unlock the door.'

'Listen, Jack,' said Susie. 'This is going to be a LOVELY tale to tell all the others at school. Won't the Secret Seven be laughed at? Silly old Secret Seven, tricked by a stupid notebook. They think themselves so grand and so clever, but they're sure that four children in a shed are a gang of robbers shooting at one another! And we only had paper bags to pop!'

The four inside popped paper bags again and roared with laughter. The Secret Seven felt gloomier and gloomier.

'You know, Susie will make everyone roar with laughter about this,' said Colin. 'We shan't be able to hold our heads up for ages. Susie's right. We'll have to let them go free, and not set on them when they come out.'

'No!' said Peter and Jack.

'*Yes*,' said Colin. 'We'll *have* to make a bargain with them, and Susie jolly well knows it. We'll have to let them go free in return for their keeping silent about this. It's no good, we've got to. *I* don't want all the silly kids in the first form roaring with laughter and popping paper bags at me whenever I go by. And they will. I know them!'

There was a silence. It dawned on everyone that Colin was right. Susie had got the best of them. They *couldn't* allow anyone to make a laughing-stock of their Secret Seven Society. They were so proud of it; it was the best Secret Society in the world.

Peter sighed. Susie *was* a pest. Somehow they must pay her back for this tiresome, aggravating trick. But for the moment she had won.

'Susie! You win, for the present!' said Peter. 'You can go free, and we won't even pull your hair, if you promise solemnly not to say a single word about this to anyone at school.'

'All right,' called Susie, triumphantly. 'I knew you'd have to make that bargain. What a swizz for you! Silly old Secret Seven! Meeting solemnly week after week with never a thing to do! Well, we're coming out, so mind you keep your word.'

The door was unlocked from inside and the four came out, laughing and grinning. They stalked through the Secret Seven, noses in the air, enjoying their triumph. Jack's fingers itched to grab at Susie's hair, but he kept them in his pockets.

'Goodbye. Thanks for a marvellous

show,' said the irritating Susie. 'Let us know when you want another adventure, and we'll provide one for you. See you later, Jack!'

They went off down the alley-way, still laughing. It was a gloomy few minutes for the Seven, as they stood in the dark yard, hearing the footsteps going down the alley.

'We MUST find something really exciting ourselves now, as soon as possible,' said Colin. 'That will stop Susie and the others jeering at us.'

'If only we could!' said Peter. 'But the more you look for an adventure the farther away it seems. Bother Susie! What a horrible evening we've had!'

But it wasn't quite the end of it. A lamp suddenly shone out nearby and a voice said:

'Now then! What are you doing here? Clear off, you kids, or I'll report you to your parents!'

It was the policeman! Well! To think they

had been turned off by the police as if *they* were a gang of robbers, and they had had such high hopes of fetching this very policeman to capture a gang in that shed! It was all very, very sad.

In deep silence the Seven left the yard and went gloomily up the alley-way. They could hardly say good night to one another. Oh, for a real adventure, one that would make them important again, and fill their days with breathless excitement!

Be patient, Secret Seven. One may be just round the corner. You just never know!

[6]

A sudden adventure

Next day Peter and Janet talked and talked about Susie's clever trick. Why, oh why, had they allowed themselves to be so easily taken in? Scamper listened sympathetically to their gloomy voices, and went first to one, then to the other, wagging his tail.

'He's trying to tell us he's sorry about it!' said Janet, with a little laugh. 'Oh, Scamper, if only we'd taken you with us, you'd have known Susie was in that shed with her silly friends, and somehow you'd have found a way of telling us.'

Scamper gave a little whine, and then lay on his back, his legs working hard, as if he were pedalling a bicycle upside down. He always did this when he wanted to make the two children laugh.

They laughed now, and patted him. Good old Scamper!

Their mother popped her head in at the door. 'Don't forget you're to go to tea with old Mrs Penton this afternoon.'

'My bike's got a puncture,' said Janet. 'It's *such* a long way to walk. Need I go?'

'Well, Daddy is going out in the car this afternoon. He can take you there, and fetch you back afterwards,' she said. 'He'll call for you about six o'clock, so mind you don't keep him waiting.'

The car was waiting outside Janet's school for her that afternoon, with Daddy at the wheel. They picked Peter up at his school gates, and Daddy drove them to Mrs Penton's. She had been their mother's old nanny, and she was very fond of them.

They forgot all about their annoyance with Susie when they saw the magnificent tea that Mrs Penton had got ready.

'Goodness – cream buns! How delicious!'

said Janet. 'And chocolate éclairs. Did Mummy like them when you were her nanny?'

'Oh yes, she ate far too many once, and I was up all night with her,' said Mrs Penton. 'Very naughty she was, that day, just wouldn't do what she was told, and finished up by over-eating. Dear, dear, what a night I had with her!'

It seemed impossible that their mother could ever have been naughty or have eaten too many cream buns and éclairs. Still, it would be a very easy thing to eat at least a dozen of them, Janet thought, looking at the lovely puffy cream oozing out of the big buns, and those éclairs! She felt very kindly towards the little girl who was now grown-up, and her own mother!

They played the big musical box after tea, and looked at Mrs Penton's funny old picture-books. Then the clock suddenly struck six.

'Gosh, Daddy said we were to be ready at

six!' said Peter, jumping up. 'Hurry up, Janet. Thank you very much, Mrs Penton, for such a smashing tea.'

Hoot – hoo—! That was their father already outside waiting for them. Mrs Penton kissed them both.

'Thank you very, very much,' said Janet. 'I *have* enjoyed myself!'

They ran down the path and climbed into the car at the back. It was quite dark, and the car's headlights shed broad beams over the road.

'Good children,' he said. 'I only had to wait half a minute.' He put in the clutch and pressed down the accelerator; the car slid off down the road. 'I've just got to call at the station for some parcels. I'll leave the car in the yard with you in it. I shan't be a minute,' he added.

They came to the station, and Daddy backed the car out of the way at one end of the station yard. He jumped out and disappeared into the lit entrance of the station.

Peter and Janet lay back on the seat, beginning to feel that they *might* have over-eaten! Janet felt sleepy and shut her eyes. Peter began to think about the evening before, and Susie's clever trick.

He suddenly heard hurried footsteps, and thought it must be his father back again. The door was quickly opened and a man got in. Then the opposite door was opened and another man sat down in the seat beside the driver's.

Peter thought his father had brought a friend with him to give him a lift, and he wondered who it was. It was dark in the station yard, and he couldn't see the other man's face at all. Then the headlights went on, and the car moved quickly out of the yard.

Peter got a really terrible shock as soon as the car passed a lamp-post. The man driving the car wasn't his father! It was somebody he didn't know at all, a man with a low-brimmed hat, and rather long hair down to his collar. Peter's father never had long hair. Whoever was this driving the car?

The boy sat quite still. He looked at the other man when they went by a lamp-post again. No, that wasn't his father either! It was a man he had never seen before. His head was bare and the hair was very short, quite different from his companion's.

A little cold feeling crept round Peter's heart. Who were these men? Were they stealing his father's car? What was he to do?

Janet stirred a little. Peter leaned over to her and put his lips right to her ear.

'Janet!' he whispered. 'Are you awake? Listen to me. I think the car is being stolen by two men, and they don't know we're at the back. Slip quietly down to the floor, so that if they happen to turn round they won't see us. Quick now, for goodness' sake!'

[7]

Something to work on

Janet was awake now, very much awake! She took one scared look at the heads of the two men in front, suddenly outlined by a street lamp, and slid quickly down to the floor. She began to tremble.

Peter slipped down beside her. 'Don't be frightened. I'll look after you. So long as the men don't know we're here, we're all right.'

'But where are they taking us?' whispered Janet, glad that the rattling of the car drowned her voice.

'I've no idea. They've gone down the main street, and now they're in a part of the town I don't know,' whispered Peter. 'Hallo, they're stopping. Keep down, Janet, and don't make a sound!'

The driver stopped the car and peered out of the open window. 'You're all right here,' he said to his companion. 'No one's about. Get in touch with Q8061 at once. Tell him Sid's place, five o'clock any evening. I'll be there.'

'Right,' said the other man and opened his door cautiously. Then he shut it again, and ducked his head down.

'What's up? Someone coming?' said the driver.

'No. I think I've dropped something,' said the other man, in a muffled voice. He appeared to be groping over the floor. 'I'm sure I heard something drop.'

'For goodness' sake! Clear out now while the going's good!' said the driver impatiently. 'The police will be on the lookout for this car in a few minutes. I'm going to Sid's, and I don't know anything at all about you, see? Not a thing!'

The other man muttered something and

opened his door again. He slid out into the dark road. The driver got out on his side; both doors were left open, as the men did not want to make the slightest noise that might call attention to them.

Peter sat up cautiously. He could not see or hear anything of the two men. The darkness had swallowed them completely. In this road the lamp-posts were few and far between, and the driver had been careful to stop in the darkest spot he could find. He had switched headlights and sidelights off as soon as he had stopped.

Peter reached over to the front of the car and switched them on. He didn't want anything to run into his father's car and smash it. He wished he could drive, but he couldn't, and anyway, he was much too young to have a licence. What should he do now?

Janet sat up, too, still trembling. 'Where are we?' she said. 'Have those men gone?'

'Yes. It's all right, Janet; I don't think they're coming back,' said Peter. 'Well, I wonder who they were and why they wanted to come here in the car? Talk about an adventure! We were moaning last night because there wasn't even the smell of one, and now here's one, right out of the blue!'

'Well, I don't much like an adventure in the dark,' said Janet. 'What are we going to do?'

'We must get in touch with Daddy,' said Peter. 'He must still be waiting at the station, unless he's gone home! But we haven't been more than a few minutes. I think I'll try to find a telephone box and telephone the station to see if Daddy is still there.'

'I'm not going to wait in the car by myself,' said Janet, at once. 'Oh dear, I wish we had Scamper with us. I should feel much better then.'

'The men wouldn't have taken the car if Scamper had been with us,' said Peter, getting out. 'He would have barked, and they would have run off to someone else's car. Come on, Janet, get out. I'll lock the doors in case there is anyone else who might take a fancy to Daddy's car!'

He locked all the doors, Janet holding his torch for him so that he could see what he was doing. Then they went down the street to see if they could find a telephone box anywhere.

They were lucky. One was at the corner of the very road where they were! Peter slipped inside and dialled the railway station.

'Station here,' said a voice at the other end.

'This is Peter, of Old Mill House,' said Peter. 'Is my father at the station still, by any chance?'

'Yes, he is,' said the voice. 'He's just collecting some parcels. Do you want to speak to him? Right, I'll ask him to come to the phone.'

Half a minute later Peter heard his father's voice. 'Yes? Who is it? *You*, Peter! But – but aren't you still in the car, in the station yard? Where are you?'

Peter explained everything as clearly as he could, and his father listened to his tale in amazement. 'Well! Two car thieves going off with my car and not guessing you and Janet were in it. Where are you?'

'Janet's just asked somebody,' said Peter. 'We're in Jackson Street, not far from the Broadway. Can you get here, Dad, and fetch the car? We'll wait.'

'Yes. I'll get a taxi here in the yard,' said his father. 'Well, of all the things to happen!'

Janet and Peter went back to the car. Now that they knew their father would be along in a few minutes they no longer felt scared. Instead they began to feel rather pleased and important.

'We'll have to call a Secret Seven meeting

about this *at once*,' said Peter. 'The police will be on to it, I expect, and *we'll* work on it too. What will Susie do *now*? Who cares about her silly tricks? Nobody at all!'

[8]

Another meeting

In a short time a taxi drew up beside the car and the children's father jumped out.

'Here we are!' called Janet, as her father paid the taxi-man.

He ran over, and got into the driver's seat. 'Well! Little did I think my car had been driven away while I was in the station,' he said. 'Are you sure you're all right?'

'Oh yes,' said Peter. 'We were half asleep at the back; the men didn't even spot us. They got in and drove straight to this place, then got out. They hardly said a word to one another.'

'Oh. Well, I suppose they weren't really car thieves,' said his father. 'Just a couple of young idiots who wanted to drive somewhere instead of walk. I shan't bother to inform the police. We'd never catch the fellows, and it would be a waste of everyone's time. I've got the car back; that's all that matters.'

The two children felt a little flat to have their extraordinary adventure disposed of in this way.

'But aren't you *really* going to tell the police?' asked Peter, quite disappointed. 'The men may be real crooks.'

'They probably are. But I'm not going to waste *my* time on them,' said his father. 'They'll be caught for something sooner or later! It's a good thing you had the sense to keep quiet in the back of the car!'

Their mother was a good deal more interested in the affair than Daddy, yet even she thought it was just a silly prank on the part of two young men. But it was different when Peter telephoned Jack and told him what happened. Jack was absolutely thrilled.

'Gosh! Really! I wish I'd been with you!' he shouted in excitement, clutching the telephone hard. 'Let's have a meeting about it. Tomorrow afternoon at three o'clock? We've all got a half-term holiday tomorrow, haven't we? We'll tell the others at school there's a meeting on. I'll . . . Sh. Sh!'

'What are you shushing about?' asked Peter. 'Oh, is that awful Susie about? All right, not a word more. See you tomorrow.'

Next afternoon, at three o'clock, all the Secret Seven were down in the shed, Scamper with them too, running from one to another excitedly. He could feel that something important was afoot!

The oil-stove was already lit and the shed was nice and warm. Curtains were drawn across the windows in case anyone should peer in. Nobody had had time to bring things to eat, but fortunately George had had a present of a large bag of humbugs from his grandmother. He handed them round.

'I say, how super,' said Jack. 'Your granny does buy such ENORMOUS humbugs. They last for ages. Now we shall all be comfortable for the rest of the afternoon, with one of these in our cheeks.'

They sat round on boxes or on old rugs, each with their cheeks bulging with a peppermint humbug. Scamper didn't like them, which was lucky. The children made him sit by the door and listen in case anyone came prying – that awful Susie, for instance, or one of her silly friends!

Peter related the whole event, and everyone listened, thrilled.

'And do you mean to say your father isn't going to the police?' said Colin. 'Well, that leaves the field free for us. Come along, Secret Seven, here's something right up our street!'

'It's very exciting,' said Pam. 'But what

exactly are we going to work on? I mean, what is there to find out? I wouldn't even know where to *begin*!'

'Well, I'll tell you what *I* think,' said Peter, carefully moving his humbug to the other cheek. 'I think those men are up to something. I don't know what, but I think we ought to find out something about them.'

'But how can we?' asked Pam. 'I don't like the sound of them, anyway.'

'Well, if you don't want to be in on this, there's nothing to stop you from walking out,' said Peter, getting cross with Pam. 'The door's over there.'

Pam changed her mind in a hurry. 'Oh no, I *want* to be in on this; of course I do. You tell us what to do, Peter.'

'Well we don't *know* very much,' said Peter. 'Excuse me, all of you, but I'm going to take my humbug out for a minute or two, while I talk. There, that's better. No,

Scamper, don't sniff at it; you don't *like* humbugs!'

With his sweet safely on a clean piece of paper beside him, Peter addressed the meeting.

'We haven't really much to go on, as I said,' he began. 'But we have a *few* clues. One is "Sid's place". We ought to try and find where that is and watch it, to see if either of the men go there. Then we could shadow them. We'd have to watch it at five o'clock each day.'

'Go on,' said George.

'Then there's Q8061,' said Peter. 'That might be a telephone number. We could find out about that.'

'That's silly!' said Pam. 'It doesn't look a bit like a telephone number!'

Peter took no notice of Pam. 'One man had a low-brimmed hat and long hair down to his collar,' he said. 'And I *think* there was something wrong with one hand – it looked as if the tip of the middle finger was missing. I only *just* caught sight of it in the light of a lamp-post, but I'm fairly sure.'

'And the other man had very short hair,' said Janet, suddenly. 'I did notice that. Oh, and Peter, do you remember that he said he thought he'd dropped something? Do you think he had? We never looked to see! He didn't find whatever it was.'

'Gosh, yes. I forgot all about that,' said Peter. 'That's most important. We'll all go and look in the car at once. Bring your torches, please, Secret Seven!'

[9]

The Seven get going

Scamper darted out into the garden with the Seven. Jack looked about to see if Susie or any of her friends were in hiding, but as Scamper didn't run barking at any bush, he felt sure that Susie must be somewhere else!

They all went to the garage. Peter hoped that the car would be there. It was! The children opened the doors and looked inside.

'It's no good us looking in the back,' said Peter. 'The men were in front.'

He felt about everywhere, and shone his torch into every corner of the front of the car. The garage was rather dark, although it was only half-past three in the afternoon.

'Nothing!' he said disappointed.

'Let *me* see,' said Janet. 'I once dropped a pencil and couldn't find it, and it was down between the two front seats!'

She slid her fingers in between the two seats and felt about. She gave a cry and pulled something out. It was a spectacle case. She held it up in triumph.

'Look! That's it. He dropped his spectacle case!'

'But he didn't wear glasses,' said Peter.

'He could have reading glasses, couldn't he?' said Janet. 'Like Granny?'

She opened the case. It was empty. She gave another little squeal.

'Look, it's got his name inside! What do you think of *that*? And his telephone number! *Now* we're on to something!'

The Secret Seven crossed round to look. Janet pointed to a little label inside. On it neatly written was a name and number: 'Briggs. Renning 2150.'

'Renning – that's not far away!' said

Peter. 'We can look up the name in the telephone directory and see his address. Gosh, what a find!'

Everyone was thrilled. Jack was just about to shut the door of the car when he suddenly remembered that no one had looked *under* the left-hand front seat, where the man who had dropped something had sat. He took a little stick from a bundle of garden bamboos standing in a nearby corner and poked under the seat with it, and out rolled a button!

'Look!' said Jack, holding it up.

Peter gave it a glance.

'Oh that's off my father's mac,' he said. 'It must have been there for ages.'

He put it into his pocket, and they all went back to the shed, feeling very excited.

'Well, first we find out Mr Briggs' address. Then we all ride over to see him,' said Peter. 'We'll make him admit he dropped it in the car, and then I'll pounce like anything and say, "And what were you doing in my father's car?" I'm sure the police would be interested if we could actually tell them the name and address of the man who went off in Dad's car like that, and probably they would make him give the name of the other man too!'

This long speech made Peter quite out of breath. The others gazed at him in admiration. It all sounded very bold.

'All right. What about now, this very minute, if we can find his address in Renning?' said Jack. 'Nothing like striking while the iron's hot. We could have tea in that little tea-shop in Renning. They have wonderful macaroons. I ate five last time I was there.'

'Then somebody else must have paid the bill,' said Colin. 'Yes, do let's go now. It *would* be fun, but you can do the talking, Peter!'

'Have you all got your bikes?' said Peter.

'Good. Let's just go in and take a look at the telephone directory, and get the address. Mr Briggs, we're coming after you!'

The telephone directory was very helpful. Mr H. E. J. Briggs lived at Little Hill, Raynes Road, Renning. Telephone number 2150. Peter copied it down carefully.

'Got enough money for tea, everyone?' he asked.

Colin had only a few pence, so Peter offered to lend him some. Now they were all ready to set off.

Peter told his mother they were going out to tea, and away they went, riding carefully in single line down the main road, as they had been taught to do.

Renning was about three miles away, and it didn't really take them long to get there.

'Shall we have tea first?' asked George, looking longingly at the tea-shop they were passing.

'No. Work first, pleasure afterwards,'

said Peter, who was always very strict about things like that. They cycled on to Raynes Road.

It was only a little lane, set with pretty little cottages. Little Hill was at one end, a nice little place with a colourful garden.

'Well it doesn't *look* like the home of a crook,' said Jack. 'But you never know. See, there's someone in the garden, Peter. Come on, do your job. Let's see how you handle things of this sort. Make him admit he dropped that spectacle case in your father's car!'

'Right!' said Peter, and went in boldly at the garden gate. 'Er – good afternoon. Are you Mr Briggs?'

[10]

Peter feels hot all over

As soon as Peter saw the man closely, he knew at once that he wasn't either of the men in the car. For one thing, this man had a big round head, and a face to match, and both the other men had had rather narrow heads, as far as he had been able to see.

The man looked a little surprised. 'No,' he said. 'I'm not Mr Briggs. I'm just a friend staying with him. Do you want him? I'll call him?'

Peter began to feel a little uncomfortable. Somehow this pretty garden and trim little cottage didn't seem the kind of place those men would live in!

'Henry! Henry, there's someone asking for you!' called the man.

Peter saw that the other Secret Seven members were watching eagerly. Would 'Henry' prove to be one of the men they were hunting for?

A man came strolling out, someone with trim, short hair and a narrow head. Yes, he *might* be the man who had sat in the left-hand seat of the car, except that he didn't in the least look as if he could possibly take someone else's car!

Still you never know! thought Peter.

The man looked inquiringly at him. 'What do you want?' he said.

'Er – is your name Mr H. E. J. Briggs, sir?' asked Peter, politely.

'It is,' said the man looking amused. 'Why?'

'Er – well, have you by any chance lost a spectacle case?' asked Peter.

All the rest of the Seven outside the garden held their breath. What would he say?

'Yes. I *have* lost one,' said the man surprised. 'Have you found it? Where was it?'

'It was in the front of a car,' answered Peter, watching him closely.

Now if the man was one of the car-thieves, he would surely look embarrassed, or deny it. He would know that it was the case he had dropped the night before and would be afraid of saying 'Yes, I dropped it there.'

'What an extraordinary thing!' said the man. 'Whose car? You sound rather *mysterious*. Losing a spectacle case is quite an ordinary thing to do, you know!'

'It was dropped in my father's car last night,' said Peter, still watching the man.

'Oh no, it wasn't,' said Mr Briggs at once. 'I've lost this case for about a week. It can't be mine. I wasn't in anyone's car last night.'

'It *is* the man we want, I bet it is!' said Pam in a low voice to Janet. 'He's telling fibs!'

'The case has your name in it,' said Peter, 'so we know it's yours. And it *was* in my father's car last night.'

'Who *is* your father?' said the man, sounding puzzled. 'I can't quite follow what you're getting at. And where's the case?'

'My father lives at Old Mill House,' began Peter, 'and he's—'

'Good gracious! He's not Jack, my farmer friend, surely?' said Mr Briggs. 'That explains everything! He very kindly gave me a lift one day last week, and I must have dropped my spectacle case in his car then. I hunted for it everywhere when I got back home. Never thought of the car, of course! Well, well, so you've brought it back?'

'Oh, are you the man my father speaks of as Harry?' said Peter, taken aback. 'Gosh! Well I suppose you *did* drop your case, then, and not last night, as I thought. Here it is. It's got your name and telephone number in it. That's how we knew it was yours.'

He held it out, and the man took it, smiling. 'Thanks,' he said, 'and now perhaps you'll tell me what all the mystery was about, and why you insisted I had dropped it last night, and why you looked at me as if I were somebody Very Suspicious Indeed.'

Peter heard the others giggling, and he went red. He really didn't know *what* to say!

'Well,' he said, 'you see, two men took my father's car last night, and when we looked in it today we found this case, and we thought perhaps it belonged to one of the men.'

Mr Briggs laughed. 'I see, doing a little detective work. Well, it's very disappointing for you, but I don't happen to be a car-thief. Look, here's five pounds for bringing back my case. Buy some chocolate and share it with those interested friends of yours watching over the hedge.'

'Oh no, thank you,' said Peter, backing

away. 'I don't want anything. I'm only too glad to bring your case back. Goodbye!'

He went quickly out of the garden, most relieved to get away from the amused eyes of Mr Briggs. Goodness, what a mistake! He got on his bicycle and rode swiftly away, the other six following.

They all stopped outside the tea-shop.

'Whew!' said Peter, wiping his forehead. 'I DID feel awful when I found out he was a friend of my father's! Dad is always talking about a man called Harry, but I didn't know his surname before.'

'We thought we were so clever, but we weren't this time,' said Colin. 'Bother! The spectacle case was nothing to do with those two men in the car, but perhaps the button is?'

'Perhaps,' said Peter. 'But I'm not tackling anyone wearing macs with buttons that match the one we found, unless I'm jolly certain he's one of those men! I feel hot all over when I think of Mr Briggs. Suppose he goes and tells my father all about this?'

'Never mind,' said Jack, grinning. 'It was great fun watching you. Let's have tea. Look, they've got macaroons today.'

In they went and had a wonderful tea. And now, what next? Think hard, Secret Seven, and make some exciting plans!

[11]

Jobs for every member

The next day another Secret Seven meeting was held, but this time it was at Colin's, in his little summer-house. It wasn't such a good place as Peter's shed, because it had an open doorway with no door, and they were not allowed to have an oil-stove in it.

However, Colin's mother had asked all the Secret Seven to tea, so it was clear they would have to have their next meeting at his house, and the little summer-house was the only place where they could talk in secret.

'We'll bring our old clothes for the Guy and decide what he should wear,' said Peter. 'We haven't even thought about him in the last two meetings and it's Bonfire Night in a few days. We'll need paper and straw for stuffing him too.'

So all the Secret Seven went to Colin's house that evening. They had a fine tea, the kind they all enjoyed most.

'Sardine sandwiches, honey sandwiches, a smashing cherry cake with cherries inside *and* on top, and an iced sponge cake. I say, Colin, your mother's a wonder,' said Peter, approvingly. 'Isn't she going to have it with us? I'd like to thank her.'

'No, she's had to go out to a committee meeting or something,' said Colin. 'All she said was that we've to behave ourselves, and if we go down to the summer-house this cold dark evening, we've GOT to put on our coats.'

'Right,' said Peter. 'Coats it will be. Mothers are always very keen on coats, aren't they? Personally, I think it's quite hot today.'

They finished up absolutely everything

on the tea-table. There wasn't even a piece of the big cherry cake left! Scamper, who had also been asked to tea, had his own dish of dog-biscuits with shrimp paste on each. He was simply delighted, and crunched them up nonstop.

'Now we'll go to the summer-house. We'd better take a candle it's so dark already,' said Colin. 'And don't forget your coats everyone.'

'And the things for the Guy,' said Peter.

So down they all went to the little wooden summer-house, carrying paper, straw, string and safety pins as well as an odd assortment of old clothes. The house had a wooden bench running all round it and felt a bit cold. Nobody minded that. It was such a nice secret place to talk in, down at the bottom of the dark garden.

The candle was stuck in a bottle and lit. There was no shelf to put it on, so Colin stood it in the middle of the floor.

'Have to be careful of Scamper knocking it over!' said Peter. 'Where is he?'

'He's gone into the kitchen to see Daddy,' said Colin. 'He's cooking a stew or something, and Scamper smelt it. He'll be along soon. Now stack your things under the wooden bench for the time being. That's right. We'll look at the clothes when we've finished the meeting.'

'We'll begin it now,' said Peter. 'Owing to our silly mistake about the spectacles case, we're not as far on with this adventure as we ought to be. We must do a little more work on it. First, has anyone any idea where "Sid's place" is?'

There was a silence.

'Never heard of it,' said Jack.

'Well, it must be some place that is used by men like those two in my father's car,' said Peter.

'Perhaps Larry at the garage would know?' said Colin, who had great faith in

Larry. 'He knows a lot of lorry-drivers, and they're the kind who might go to some place called "Sid's" or "Jim's" or "Nick's".'

'Yes. That's a good idea,' said Peter. 'Colin, you and George go and find out from Larry tomorrow. Now, what else can we do? What about the number that one of the men had to get in touch with – what was it now?'

'Q8061,' said Pam, promptly. 'I think of it as the *letter* Q, but it might be spelt K-E-W, you know.'

'Yes, you're right. It might,' said Peter. 'That's really quite an idea, Pam. It might be a number at Kew telephone exchange, Kew 8061. You and Barbara can make it your job to find out.'

'How do we set about it?' said Barbara.

'I really can't explain such easy things to you,' said Peter, impatiently. 'You and Pam can quite well work out what to do yourselves. Now is there anything else we can work on?'

'Only the button we found in the car,' said Jack.

'I told you, it's sure to belong to my father's mac,' said Peter. 'It's just like the buttons on it.'

'But we ought to make *sure*,' argued Jack. 'You know you always say we never ought to leave anything to chance, Peter. There are hundreds of different coat buttons.'

'Well, perhaps you're right,' said Peter. 'Yes, I think you are. Janet, will you see to that point, please, and look at Dad's mac. I know he's got a button missing, so I expect it belongs to his mac, but we *will* make sure.'

'You haven't given *me* anything to do,' said Jack.

'Well, if the button doesn't match the ones on Dad's mac, you can take charge of *that* point,' said Peter, with a sudden giggle, 'and you can march about looking for people wearing a mac with a missing button.'

'Don't be an idiot,' said Jack. 'Still, if it *isn't* your father's button, it *will* be one dropped by one of those men, and one of us ought to take charge of it. So I will, if it's necessary.'

'Right,' said Peter. 'Well, that's the end of the meeting. Now let's think about the Guy.'

[12]

Oh, what a pity!

Colin and Jack took the bundles of clothes for the Guy out from under the wooden bench of the summer-house. The Seven knelt down on the floor to sort everything out. What a lovely job!

'I wish we had a better light than just this flickering candle on the floor,' said Pam. 'It's difficult to see what colour the clothes are.'

Colin pulled out a fearsome-looking mask from the pile of old things. 'Who brought this? It looks like the villain in that play we saw on TV last night.' He put on the mask and hissed menacingly: your money or your life.'

'You look worse than that villain, Colin,'

said Janet. 'I got the mask at a party ages ago and I put it away for Guy Fawkes. I almost forgot where I had put it.'

'It will make a really frightening Guy. I can just imagine him leering down at us from the top of the bonfire,' said Barbara.

'We'd better start making the Guy,' said Peter. 'This is a good big pair of trousers. If we stuff straw and screwed up paper down the legs we can safety pin those old slippers on the bottoms to look like feet.'

'And here's your father's old green jacket, George. We can do the same to the arms and pin my old gloves on for hands,' said Barbara, 'though his hands will look a bit smaller than the rest of him!'

'Look what I've brought,' said Pam. 'I thought it would be much easier to have an old cushion for a body instead of straw and paper. Mother said I could take this old blue one that has been leaking stuffing.'

The Secret Seven began to roll up paper

and stuff straw into the trousers and jacket. It was difficult to see what they were doing with only the light of the candle. As they worked, they heard the sound of a bark, and then scampering feet. Scamper had been let out of the kitchen door and was coming to find his friends. Where were they? Wuff! Wuff!

'Scamper!' called Janet from the summer-house. 'We're here!'

Scamper tore down the garden path, barking madly. Anyone would think he had been away from the seven children for a whole month, not just half an hour!

He rushed straight into the little summer-house and over went the bottle with the lit candle in its neck! Crash!

'You idiot, Scamper,' said Peter and reached to set the bottle upright again. The candle was still alight.

But before he could take hold of it, the

flame of the candle had licked against a bundle of straw. It was alight!

'Fire!' yelled Peter. 'Look out, Pam! Look out, Barbara!'

The straw flared up and the loose paper on the floor began to burn too. The children tried to stamp out the flames but the fire spread faster than they could stamp.

Flames licked at the wooden bench. The old clothes were smouldering, sending out black smoke that made the children cough and splutter.

The seven children hurried out of the little summer-house clutching each other. Scamper, really terrified, had completely disappeared.

They all turned to look back. Fire glowed through the doorway and windows. They could hear a crackling as their things burned.

'We'd better get some water,' said Colin, suddenly. 'The summer-house will catch fire and burn down. Quick!'

They left the fire and ran to get buckets. There was a little pond nearby, and they filled the buckets from it. Splash! Splash! Splash! The water was thrown all over the summer-house, and there was a tremendous sizzling noise. Black smoke poured out of the little house and almost choked the Seven.

'Pooh!' said Jack, and coughed. 'What a horrible smell!'

'It's a good thing your father didn't see this,' panted Peter to Colin, coming up with another pail of water. 'He would be furious about this. There, I think we've about got the fire down now. POOOOOH! That smoke!'

It was a very, very sad ending to the tea and meeting at Colin's. Barbara was in tears. There was nothing left of the Guy but smoke and smell and a nasty-looking black mess.

'It's bad luck,' said Peter, feeling as if he

wouldn't mind howling himself. 'Bother Scamper! It's all his fault. Where is he?'

'Gone home at sixty miles an hour, I should think,' said Janet. 'It's a pity he hasn't got a post-office savings book like we have. I'd make him take some money out and buy another mask for us.'

'We'll have to see if we can collect some more clothes. But I don't suppose people will want to give us any more after this,' said George.

'I hope your parents won't be too cross about the summer-house,' said Jack gloomily. 'At least it didn't burn down, but everything is very black and wet. The wooden bench is a bit charred too. I'll come along tomorrow, when it's dried up a bit, and help you to clear it up.'

They were just about to go off to the front gate when Janet stopped them. 'We meant to choose a new password today,' she said. 'You know that Susie knows our last one,

"Guy Fawkes", and we really *must* have a secret one. Susie has told everyone in our class.'

'Yes. I forgot about that,' said Peter. 'Well, I vote we have "Bonfire". It really does seem a very good password for to-night!'

'All right – Bonfire,' said Colin. 'I'm sorry it's been such a disappointing evening. This is definitely *not* the kind of adventure I like! Goodbye, all of you. See you tomorrow!'

It was a gloomy company of children that made their way home. Bother Scamper, *why* did he have to do a silly thing like that?

[13]

Sid's Place

All the Secret Seven felt exceedingly gloomy next day, which was Sunday. They met at Sunday School, but none of them had much to say. They were all very subdued. Colin's parents had been very cross about the damaged summer-house and had forbidden him ever to use candles there again.

'Scamper *did* race home last night,' said Janet to the girls. 'He was behind the couch, trembling from head to foot. He is awfully frightened of fire you know.'

'Poor Scamper!' said Pam. 'Did you forgive him?'

'We simply had to,' said Janet. 'Anyway, he didn't mean to upset the candle, poor Scamper. We stroked him and patted him and loved him, and when he saw we weren't going to scold him, he crept out and sat as close to our legs as he could, and put his head on my knee.'

'He's so sweet,' said Barbara. 'But all the same it's *dreadful* to have lost our Guy.'

'It's quite put our adventure out of my mind,' said Pam. 'But I suppose we'd better think about it again tomorrow, Barbara. We've got to find out about that telephone number, Kew 8061. Though how we shall do it, I don't know.'

'Leave it till tomorrow,' said Barbara. 'I can't think of anything but our poor Guy today.'

The next day was Monday, and the Seven were back at school. George and Colin went to call at the garage after morning school, to try and find out something about 'Sid's Place' from Larry. He was sitting in a corner with a newspaper, munching his lunch.

'Hallo, Larry,' said Colin. 'I wonder if you can help us. Do you know anywhere called "Sid's Place"?'

'No, I don't,' said Larry. 'Sounds like an eating-house or something. There's a lorry-driver coming in soon. If you'd like to wait, I'll ask him.'

The lorry drove in after three or four minutes, and the man got down, a big heavy fellow who called out cheerfully to Larry. 'Just off to get a bite of dinner. Be back in half an hour for my lorry.'

'Hey, Charlie, do you eat at "Sid's Place"?' called Larry. 'Do you know it?'

' "Sid's Place"? No, I eat at my sister's when I come through here,' said Charlie. 'Wait a minute now. "Sid's" you said. Yes I remember seeing a little café called "Sid's Café". Would that be the place you're meaning?'

'Could be,' said Larry, looking questioningly at Colin.

Colin nodded. 'Probably the one,' he said, feeling suddenly excited. 'Where is it?'

'You know Old Street? Well, it's at the corner of Old Street and James Street, not a first-class place, and not the sort you boys want to go to. So long, Larry. See you in half an hour!'

'Thanks, Larry,' said Colin. 'Come on, George, let's go and have a look at this place. We've just about got time.'

They went to Old Street and walked down to James Street at the end. On the corner, sharing a bit of each street, was a rather dirty-looking eating-house. 'Sid's Café' was painted over the top of the very messy window.

The boys looked inside. Men were sitting at a long counter, eating sandwiches and drinking coffee or tea. There were one or two tables in the shop, too, at which slightly better-dressed men were having a hot meal served to them by a fat and cheerful girl.

'Oh so that's "Sid's Place",' said Colin, staring in. 'I wonder which is Sid?'

'Perhaps Sid is somewhere in the back quarters,' said George. 'There are only girls serving here. Well we know that one of those men comes here every day about five o'clock. One of us must watch, and we'll be bound to see the man.'

'It'll have to be Peter,' said Colin. 'We wouldn't know the man. He would probably recognise him at once.'

'Yes. It's going to be very difficult for him to hang about here, watching everyone,' said George. 'People will wonder what he's up to. Two of us would seem even *more* suspicious.'

'Well that's up to Peter!' said Colin. 'We've done *our* job and found Sid's place. Come on, we'll be awfully late for lunch.'

Peter was very pleased with Colin and George when he heard their news. 'Good work!' he said. 'I'll get along there at five o'clock this afternoon. How have Pam and Barbara got on?'

Janet told him while they had a quick tea together after afternoon school. 'They just couldn't think *how* to do anything about KEW 8061,' said Janet. 'They simply couldn't.'

'Couple of idiots!' said Peter, munching a bun quickly. 'Hurry up, I must go.'

'Well, Pam asked her mother how to find out if there *was* such a number, because she and Barbara really didn't feel they could wade all through the telephone directories,' said Janet. 'And her mother said, "Well, just ring up and see if there's an answer!"'

'Easy,' said Peter. 'Simple!'

'Yes – well, they rang up the number, feeling very excited, because they thought they could ask whoever answered what his name and address were, but there was no reply,' said Janet. 'And the operator said it was because there was no telephone with that number at present! So Q8061 is *not* a telephone number, Peter. It must be something else!'

'Bother!' said Peter, getting up. 'It would have been marvellous if KEW 8061 *had* answered. We'd have been able to get the name and address and everything. That clue isn't much good, I'm afraid. I must be off, Janet. Wouldn't it be wonderful if I spotted one of the men going into Sid's place?'

'It *would*,' said Janet. 'Oh, I DO hope you do, Peter!'

[14]

A wonderful idea

Peter went as quickly as he could to the corner of Old Street and James Street. Yes – there was Sid's Café, just as Colin had said. What was the time?

He glanced at his watch – six minutes to five. Well, if the man came at five o'clock, he ought just to catch him. Of course, he might come any time after that. That would be a nuisance, because then Peter would have to wait about a long time.

Peter lolled against the corner, watching everyone who came by, especially, of course, the men who went in and out of 'Sid's Café'. They were mostly men with barrows of fruit that they left outside, or drivers of vans, or shifty-looking men, unshaved and dirty.

He got a shock when someone came out of the café and spoke roughly to him.

'Now then, what are you doing here, lolling about? Don't you dare take fruit off my barrow! I've caught you boys doing it before, and I'll call the police if you do. Clear off!'

'I wouldn't *dream* of taking your fruit!' said Peter, indignantly, looking at the pile of cheap fruit on the nearby barrow.

'Ho, you wouldn't, would you? Well, then, what are you standing here for, looking about? Boys don't stand at corners for nothing! We've been watching you from inside the shop, me and my mates, and we know you're after something!'

Peter was shocked. How dare this man say things like that to him! Still, perhaps some boys did steal from barrows or from fruit-stalls outside shops.

'Go on, you tell me what you're standing about here for,' said the man again, putting his face close to Peter's.

As the boy couldn't tell him the reason why he was standing at that corner, he said nothing, but turned and went off, his face burning red. Horrible man! he thought. And I haven't seen anyone yet in the least like that man who went off in our car. Of course, all I've got to go on really is his hat and long hair, and possibly maimed finger on his right hand.

He ran back home, thinking hard. After all, that man might go to Sid's place each night and I'd *never* know him if he had a cap instead of a hat, and had cut his hair shorter. And most of these men slouch along with their hands in their pockets, so I wouldn't see his hand either. It's hopeless.

Peter went round to see Colin about it. Jack and George were there, doing their homework together.

'Hallo!' they said, in surprise. 'Aren't you

watching at Sid's place?'

Peter told them what had happened. 'I don't see how I can go and watch there any more,' he said, rather gloomily. 'That man who spoke to me was really nasty. And how can I watch without being seen?'

'Can't be done,' said Colin. 'Give it up! This is something we just can't do. Come on out to the summer-house and see what I've made! We cleared away the mess from the fire, and I've got something else there now!'

They all went out to the summer-house, with their torches. Colin shone his on to something there, and Peter jumped in astonishment, not at first realising what it was.

'Gosh! It's a Guy!' he said, in admiration. 'What a beauty!'

The Guy certainly was very fine. He was stuffed with straw, and wore some of Colin's very old clothes. He had a mask, of course, and grinned happily at the three boys. He had a wig made of black strands of wool and an old hat on top. Colin had sat him in a garden barrow, and he really looked marvellous.

'He's not man-sized because I only had my very old and small suit, but he's the best I could do,' said Colin. 'I bought another mask with my pocket money. Dad said we can have a bonfire at the bottom of the garden as long as he is there. You can all come and help build it tomorrow.'

The Guy seemed to watch them as they talked, grinning away merrily.

'It's a pity *he* can't watch outside Sid's place!' said Jack. 'Nobody would suspect him or bother about *him*. He could watch for that fellow all evening!'

They all laughed. Then Peter stopped suddenly and gazed hard at the Guy. An idea had come to him, a really WONDERFUL idea!

'Hey!' he said, clutching at Colin and making him jump. 'You've given me an idea! What about ME dressing up as a Guy, and wearing a mask with eye-holes – and one of you taking me somewhere near Sid's Café? There are heaps of these Guys about now, and nobody would think our Guy was *real*. I would watch for ages and nobody would guess.'

'Whew!' said the other three together, and stared at Peter in admiration.

Colin thumped him on the back. 'That's a brilliant idea!' he said. 'Super! Smashing! When shall we do it?'

'Tomorrow,' said Peter. 'I can rush here and dress up easily enough, and one of you can wheel me off in the barrow – all of you, if you like! What a game!'

'But my mother doesn't like the idea of children taking Guys and begging for money,' said Colin, remembering. 'She says that begging is wrong.'

'So it is,' said Peter. 'My mother says that too, but if we *did* get any money we could give it to a charity.'

'Oh well, that's all right, then!' said Colin. 'Gosh, this is grand! Mind you don't leap up out of the barrow if you see that fellow going into Sid's place, Peter!'

'I'll keep as still as a real Guy!' said Peter, grinning. 'Well, so long. See you at school tomorrow.'

[15]

The peculiar Guy

Peter raced home to tell Janet of the new idea. She was so thrilled that she couldn't say a word. What an idea! How super! She stared in admiration at her brother. He was truly a fine leader for the Secret Seven!

Scamper wuffed loudly, exactly as if he were saying, 'Great, Peter, splendid idea!'

'*I've* got something to tell you, too,' said Janet, suddenly remembering. 'I looked on Daddy's mac and he *has* got a button missing; but it's a small one on his sleeve, not a large one like we found. And also it's not quite the same colour, Peter.'

'Ah, good! That means it probably *was* a button that dropped from that man's mac!' said Peter, pleased. 'Jack will have to take the button, Janet, and work on that clue, if he can! So give it to me, and I'll hand it to him tomorrow.'

'I wish we could find out about Q8061,' said Janet. 'I'm pretty sure it must be someone's telephone number, but it's very difficult to find out.'

'There's Mother calling,' said Peter. 'I bet it's to tell me to do my homework!'

It was of course, and poor Peter found it very difficult indeed to work out arithmetic problems when his head was full of dressing up as a Guy!

All the Secret Seven were thrilled to hear of Peter's new plan, and next evening they were round at Colin's to see him dress up. He really did look remarkably good!

He wore an old pair of patched trousers, and a ragged jacket. He wore a pair of great big boots thrown out by Colin's father. He had a scarf round his neck, and a big old hat over a wig made of black wool.

'You look quite *dreadful*!' said Janet, with a giggle. 'Put the mask on now.'

Peter put it on, and immediately became a grinning Guy, like all the other Guys that were appearing here and there in the streets of the town. Scamper took one look at Peter's suddenly changed face, and backed away, growling.

'It's all right, Scamper,' said Peter, laughing. 'It's me! Don't be afraid.'

'You look horrible,' said Pam. 'I really feel scared when I look at you, though I know you're really Peter. Nobody, *nobody* could possibly guess you were alive!'

Peter got into the barrow. 'Gosh, it's very hard and uncomfortable,' he said. 'Got any old cushions, Colin?'

Colin produced an old rug and three rather dirty garden cushions. These made the barrow much more comfortable. Peter got in and lolled on the cushions in the limp, floppy way of all Guys. He really looked extremely Guy-like!

The others shrieked with laughter to see him.

'Come on,' said Colin at last. 'We really must go, or we shan't be there till long past five.'

The three boys set off, taking turns at wheeling Peter in the barrow. He kept making horrible groans and moans, and Jack laughed so much that he had to sit down on a bus-stop seat and hold his aching sides.

An old lady there peered at the Guy. 'What a good one!' she said, and fumbled in her purse. 'I'll give you some money for fireworks.'

'Oh, any money we get is going to charity,' explained George quickly.

She gave him fifty pence, and then, as the bus came up, waved to them and got on.

'How nice of her!' said George. 'Fifty whole pence.'

They went on down the street, with Peter thoroughly enjoying himself! He lolled about, watching everything through the eye-slits of his mask, and made silly remarks in a hollow Guy-like voice that made the others laugh helplessly.

At last they came to Sid's Café. The barrow was neatly wedged into a little alcove near the door, from which Peter could see everyone who went in or out.

The boys stood nearby, waiting to see if Peter recognised anyone. If he did, he was to give a sign, and two of the Seven would shadow the man to see where he went, if he happened to come *out* of the café. If he went inside it they were to wait till he came out.

The men going in and out of the eating-house were amused with the Guy. One prodded him hard with his stick, and gave Peter a terrible shock. 'Good Guy you've got there!' said the man and threw five pence on to Peter's tummy.

'Colin! Jack! You're NOT to let people prod me like that,' said Peter, in a fierce whisper. 'It really hurt.'

'Well, how are we to stop them?' said Colin, also in a whisper.

All went well till two young men came by and saw the Guy sitting there. 'Hallo! He's a good Guy!' said one. 'Nice pair of boots he's got. I've a good mind to take them off him!'

And to Peter's horror, he felt the boots on his feet being tugged hard. He gave a yell, and the young men looked extremely startled. They disappeared quickly.

'CAN'T you look after me better?' said Peter to the others. 'Heave me up a bit on the cushions. Those men pulled me off.'

Colin and George heaved him into a more comfortable position.

'Anyway, you've made quite a bit of money,' said George, in Peter's ear. 'People think you're jolly good, we've got quite a few pounds.'

Peter grunted. He was cross with the others. Why didn't they guard him from pokes and prods and pullings? Then, quite suddenly, he caught sight of somebody, and stiffened all over.

Surely, SURELY, that was one of the men who had taken his father's car? Peter stared and stared. Was it? Oh, why didn't he stand a bit nearer so that he could see?

[16]

The two men

The man was standing by the window of the café, as if he were waiting for someone. He had on a hat and his hair was rather long. Peter looked as closely at him as he could.

The man who drove the car had a low-brimmed hat, he thought, and long hair. This man somehow *looks* like that man we saw in the car.

The man moved a little nearer, and coughed impatiently. He took a handkerchief from his pocket and blew his nose. The top of one middle finger was missing. Peter knew for *certain* that it was the man he was looking for! It *must* be the man! Perhaps he's waiting for the other man.

Almost before he had finished thinking

this, the second man came up! There was no mistaking that cap and the short, cropped hair, grown a little longer now. The cap was pulled down over his face exactly as it had been when he was in the car. He wore an old mac, and Peter tried to see if it had a button missing.

The two men said a word of greeting and then went into the café. They went right through the room to a door at the back, opened it, and disappeared.

'Colin! George! Jack! Those were the two men,' called Peter in a low voice full of excitement. 'One of them had half a finger missing. I saw it.'

'And the other had a button off his mac!' said Jack. 'I noticed that, though I didn't know he was one of the men we're after! But seeing that I'm in charge of the button now, I'm making a point of looking carefully at every mac I see! I believe our button matches his exactly.'

'Good work!' said Peter. 'Now listen. The next move is very, very important. Two of you must shadow these men. If they separate, you must separate too, and each go after one of them. Colin, you must wheel me home.'

'Right,' said the three, always willing to obey Peter's leadership. He really was very good at this kind of thing.

'Get as close to those men as you can and see if you can hear anything useful,' said Peter. 'And track them right to their homes if you can. Report to me at the Secret Seven shed as soon as you can.'

'Right,' said George and Jack, feeling as if they were first-class plain-clothes policemen!

The two men were not long in Sid's. They came out after about ten minutes, looking angry. They stood in the doorway, taking no notice of the Guy and the boys.

'Sid's let us down,' said the man with the

missing finger. 'He said he'd give us two hundred and now he's knocked it down to fifty. Better go back to Q's and tell him. He'll be wild.'

The boys listened intently, pretending to fiddle about with the Guy.

'I'm not arguing with Sid again,' said the other man. 'I reckon I'm an idiot to come out of hiding, yet, till my hair's grown. Come on, let's go.'

They went off down the street, and George and Jack immediately set off behind them, leaving Colin with Peter.

'Did you hear that?' said Peter, in great excitement, forgetting he was a Guy. 'They've stolen something and want to sell it to Sid, and he won't give them what he promised. So they're going back to Q, whoever he is, probably the chief, to report it. Well we know that Q is a man, now!'

'And did you hear what the other man said about his hair growing?' said Colin, bending over Peter. 'I bet he's just come out of prison, it's so short. They always shave it there, don't they? Or perhaps he's an *escaped* prisoner, in hiding. Gosh, Peter, this is super!'

'Wheel me to our shed,' commanded Peter, wishing he could get out and walk. 'Hurry up. The girls will be there already, and George and Jack will join us as soon as they can. Do hurry up! . . . I'm going to get out and walk,' announced Peter. 'It's a nice dark road we're in. Stop a minute, Colin, and I'll get out.'

Colin stopped, and Peter climbed out of the barrow. Colin shone his torch to help him, and an old man with a dog saw the Guy stepping out of the barrow. He stared as if he couldn't believe his eyes, and then hurried off at top speed. Good gracious! A Guy coming alive. No, surely his eyes must have deceived him!

It wasn't long before Colin and Peter

were whispering the password outside the shed at the bottom of Peter's garden. The barrow was shoved into some bushes, and Peter had taken off his mask.

'Bonfire!' said the boys, and the door opened at once. Pam gave a little scream as Peter came in, still looking very peculiar with a black wool wig, an old hat, and very ragged clothes.

'We've got news!' said Peter. 'Great news. Just listen, all of you!'

[17]

Good work!

Peter quickly told the girls all that had happened, and they listened in silence, feeling very thrilled. Now they were really finding out something, even that button had helped!

'I think the short-haired man has either just come out of prison or escaped from it,' said Peter. 'He may have committed a robbery before he went in, and have hidden what he stole, and it's these goods he and the other man are trying to sell to Sid.'

'Well, who's Q, then?' asked Janet. 'Where does *he* come in?'

'He's probably holding the stolen goods,' said Peter, working everything out in his mind. 'And I expect he's sheltering the thief, too. If only we could find out who Q is and where he lives. He's the missing link.'

The five of them talked and talked, and Scamper listened and joined in with a few wuffs now and again, thumping his tail on the ground when the chatter got very loud.

'When will George and Jack be back?' asked Pam. 'I ought not to be too late home, and it's a quarter past six now!'

'Here they are!' said Colin, hearing voices outside. A knock came at the door.

'Password!' shouted everyone.

'Bonfire!' said two voices, and in went George and Jack, beaming all over their faces, glad to be out of the cold, dark November night.

'What happened? Did you shadow them?' demanded Peter, as they sat down on boxes.

'Yes,' said George. 'We followed them all the way down the street, and away by the canal and up by Cole Square. We only once got near enough to hear them say anything.'

'What was that?' asked Peter.

'One of them said "Is that a policeman lying in wait for us over there? Come on, run for it!"' said George. 'And just as a bobby came out of the shadows they ran round the corner, and the policeman never even noticed them! We shot after them, just in time to see them trying the handles of some cars parked there.'

'Then they slid quickly into one and drove off,' finished Jack. 'That was the end of our shadowing.'

'So they stole *another* car!' said Colin.

'You didn't take the number by any chance, did you?' asked Peter.

'Of course!' said Jack, and took out his notebook. 'Here it is, PLK 100. We didn't go back and tell the policeman. We thought we'd race back here and let you decide what we ought to do next.'

'Good work,' said Peter, pleased. 'If only we knew where Q lived, we'd know where the men were, and could tell the police to go and grab them there. They'd get the stolen goods too. I bet they're being held by our mysterious Q!'

'I know! I know!' suddenly yelled Pam, making everyone jump. 'Why can't we look up all the names beginning with Q in our local telephone directory? If Q lives somewhere here, his name would be there, and his number.'

'Yes but there might be a lot of Qs, and we wouldn't know which was the right one,' objected Janet. 'Why, we ourselves know a Mrs Queen, a Mr Quigley and a Miss Quorn.'

'But don't you see what I *mean*!' said Pam, impatiently. 'We'll go down all the list of Qs, and the one with the telephone number of 8061 will be *our* Q! Don't you *see*?'

Everyone saw what she meant at once.

Peter looked at Pam admiringly. 'That's a very good idea, Pam,' he said. 'I've sometimes thought that you're not as good a Secret Seven member as the others are, but now I know you are. That's a Very Good Idea. Why didn't we think of it before instead of messing about with KEW?'

'I'll get our telephone directory with all the numbers in,' said Janet and raced off.

She soon came back, gave the password and joined the others. She opened the book at the Qs, and everyone craned to look at them.

There were not very many. 'Quant,' read Pam, 'telephone number 6015. Queen, 6453, Quelling, 4322, Quentin, 8061 . . .! That's it. Look, here it is, Quentin, 8061, Barr's Warehouse, East End. Why, that's only about two miles away, right at the other end of the town.'

'Gosh!' said Peter, delighted. 'That's given us JUST the information we wanted. A warehouse, too. A fine place for hiding stolen goods! My goodness, we've done some excellent work. Pam, you deserve a pat on the back!'

She got plenty of pats, and sat back, beaming. 'What do we do now?' she said.

Before anyone could answer, there came the sound of footsteps down the path, and Peter's mother's voice called loudly: 'Peter! Janet! Are Colin and George there, and Pam? Their mothers have just telephoned to say they really must come home at once, it's getting late!'

'Okay!' called Peter. 'Wait for us. We've got a wonderful tale to tell you! Do wait!'

But his mother had gone scurrying back to the house, not liking the cold, damp evening. The seven children tore after her, with Scamper barking his head off.

Just as they went in at the back of the house, there came a knock at the front door.

'See who that is, Peter!' called his mother. 'I've got a cake in the oven I must look at.'

Peter went to the door, with the others close behind him. A big policeman stood there. He smiled at the surprised children.

'I've just been to Jack's house,' he said, 'and Susie told me he might be here. I saw you tonight in Cole Square – you and this other boy here. Well, not long after that somebody reported to me that their car had been stolen near where you were, and I wondered if either of you had noticed anything suspicious going on.'

'Oh, come in, come in!' cried Peter, joyfully. 'We can tell you a whole lot about the thieves, and we can even tell you where you'll probably find the car. Come in, do!'

[18]

Don't worry, Secret Seven!

The policeman went into the hall, looking extremely surprised. Peter's mother came from the kitchen and Peter's father looked out of his study.

'What's all this?' he said. 'Nobody has got into trouble, surely?'

'No,' said Peter. 'Oh, Daddy, you must just listen to our tale. It's really super!'

They all went into the study, the policeman looking more and more puzzled.

'I *think* you'll find that stolen car outside Barr's Warehouse, at the East End of the town,' said Peter. 'And in the warehouse you'll probably find a Mr Quentin, and quite a lot of stolen goods on the premises.'

'And you'll find a man with half a finger

missing, and another whose hair is so short that he looks like an escaped prisoner,' put in Colin.

'Wait! Wait a minute! What's this about a man with a missing half-finger?' said the policeman, urgently. 'We're looking for him – Fingers, he's called, and he's a friend of a thief who's just been in prison. He escaped last week, and we thought he might go to Fingers for help, so we've been keeping an eye open for him too.'

'They met at Sid's Café,' said Peter, enjoying everyone's astonishment.

'WHAT?' said his father. 'Sid's Café? That horrible place! Don't dare to tell me you boys have been in there.'

'Not inside, only outside,' said Peter. 'It's all right, we *really* haven't done anything wrong. It all began with that night when you left Janet and me in your car in the station yard, and two men got in and drove it away.'

'And we wanted you to go to the police, but you didn't think you'd bother,' said Janet. 'So we've been trying to trace the two men ourselves, and we have!'

Then the whole of the story came out. how they found Sid's Café, how Peter dressed up as a Guy to watch for the men, how they saw Fingers with his missing half-finger, and how George and Jack followed them and saw them steal the car near Cole Square.

'And we know where they've gone, because they have a friend called Q, a Mr Quentin,' said Peter. 'They mentioned his telephone number, it was 8061, and we looked up the number and found the address. We only did that a little while ago, actually. The address is Barr's Warehouse, as we said.'

'Amazing!' said the policeman, scribbling fast in his notebook. 'Incredible! Do these kids do this kind of thing often?'

'Well, you're a fairly new man here,' said Peter's father, 'or you'd know how they keep poking their noses into all sorts of things. I don't know that I really approve of it, but they certainly have done some good work.'

'We're the Secret Seven Society, you see,' explained Janet. 'And we really do like some kind of adventurous job to do.'

'Well, thanks very much,' said the policeman, getting up. 'I'll get a few men and ask the Sergeant to come along with us and see what we can find in Barr's Warehouse. You'll deserve a jolly good Bonfire Night tomorrow! I hope you've got a wonderful collection of fireworks, you deserve the best!'

'Our families are joining together for a big bonfire party. We all saved up for the fireworks and Colin's father is keeping them for us – though I expect all our fathers will take turns letting them off!'

'Well, have a good evening then – and mind you all take care not to get too close!' said the policeman, going to the door. 'I'm much obliged to you all. Good night!'

'What a tale!' said Peter's mother. 'I never heard of such goings-on! Whatever will you Seven do next? To think of you dressing up as a Guy, Peter, and watching outside Sid's Café! No wonder you look SO DREADFUL! Take that black wig off, do!'

'*Can't* the others stay and have a bit of supper?' Peter begged her. 'We've got such a lot to talk about. Do let them. Sandwiches will do. We'll all help to make them.'

'Very well,' said his mother, laughing at all the excited faces. 'Janet, go and telephone everybody's mothers and tell them where they are!'

The Seven were very pleased. In fifteen minutes' time they were all sitting down to potted meat sandwiches, oatmeal biscuits, apples and hot cocoa, talking nineteen to the dozen, with a very excited Scamper tearing round their legs under the table. What an unexpected party! thought Scamper, delighted, and what a wonderful selection of titbits!

The telephone suddenly rang, and Peter went to answer it. It proved to be a very exciting call indeed! He came racing back to the others.

'That was that policeman! He thought we'd like to know what happened.'

'What? Tell us!' cried everyone.

'Well, the police went to Barr's Warehouse and the first thing they saw in the yard was the stolen car!' said Peter. 'Then they forced their way in at the back door, and found Mr Quentin, scared stiff, in his office. When they told him they knew that Fingers and the escaped prisoner were somewhere in the warehouse, he just crumpled up!'

'Have they got the others?' asked Colin.

'Oh yes. Quentin showed the police where they were hiding,' said Peter. 'Down in a cellar, and the stolen goods were there too. It was a wonderful raid! By the way, the police want to know if we can identify the second man, the close-cropped man, and I said yes, if he was wearing a mac with a missing button, because we've got the button!'

'Goody, goody!' said Barbara. 'So we have. We forgot to tell the policeman about that! Where *is* the button?'

'Here,' said Jack, and spun it on the table. 'Good old button, you did your bit too! Gosh, this is one of the most exciting jobs the Secret Seven have ever done. I'm jolly sorry it's ended.'

So was everyone. They didn't want that exciting evening to come to a finish, but they had to say goodbye at last.

'Tomorrow is Bonfire Night,' said Peter to Janet as they shut the front door on the others. 'We'll all have a wonderful party and Colin's Guy will look down on us all from the top of the bonfire.'

'Shall we put you there instead, Peter? You'd look even better!' said Janet, smiling.

'I'd much rather watch the Guy than be him tomorrow night,' said Peter, 'though it was exciting being a Guy just for one night! Come on, Janet, let's go up to bed and dream about all those super fireworks . . .'

They both ran upstairs shouting at the tops of their voices, 'Bang! Whoosh! Bang-Bang-Bang!'

Enid Blyton

THE

FAMOUS FIVE'S

SURVIVAL GUIDE

Packed with useful information on surviving outdoors and solving mysteries, here is the one mystery that the Famous Five never managed to solve. See if you can follow the trail to discover the location of the priceless Royal Dragon of Siam.

The perfect book for all fans of mystery, adventure and the Famous Five!

ISBN 9780340970836

Read the first exciting collection of Secret Seven adventures:

The Secret Seven

The Secret Seven super sleuths are on the trail of a mystery. Dressed in disguise they follow a lead to a spooky old house in the snow . . .

Secret Seven Adventure

When a priceless pearl necklace goes missing the Secret Seven are first off the mark to catch the thief!

Well Done, Secret Seven

The gang have a new meeting place – a treehouse! But someone else is using it too. The Secret Seven are furious, until they learn that the intruder desperately needs their help.

Read the next exciting collection of Secret Seven adventures:

Secret Seven Win Through

The gang have a new meeting place, but someone else is using it too. How dare they? They are determined to catch this cheeky intruder, no matter what it takes!

Three Cheers, Secret Seven

When Peter and Jack go looking for their model aeroplane in an old abandoned house, they find a lit fire in one of the rooms. So, who is living there, and why?

Secret Seven Mystery

A girl has mysteriously run away from home and her parents are frantic with worry. Can the gang follow the clues and catch up with her?

READ THE FIRST EXCITING COLLECTION OF FAMOUS FIVE ADVENTURES:

Five On A Treasure Island

A Shipwreck off Kirrin Island! But where is the treasure? When searching for clues, the Famous Five realise they're not alone!

Five Go Adventuring Again

A thief at Kirrin Cottage! Who can it be? The Famous Five think they know – but they need proof! Then they find an old map and an unusual hiding place . . .

Five Run Away Together

Who's been on George's island? And what is locked in the mysterious trunk hidden on Kirrin Island? The Famous Five think they're on the trail of smugglers – until they hear a child scream . . .